READING JEFF CANNON

I've learned to read Jeff Cannon; First a read through to get the general feel of the poem, then I go back and do a line-by-line slow read to try and get an idea of the poet's feeling/motivation to have written these, invariably, graphic images of pain, mourning and revulsion that, to me, are reminiscent of the work of José Clemente Orozco.

"Day and night dance together in the silence of a desire that sought more than a sip of pleasure"

When he launches against the dark soul of the "Caucasoid empire", he does not pull back the punches, which, by the way, are not sterile or blind rage expressions of innocence lost or nostalgic feelings for a life that is no more. Jeff is as relentless as the sick system he indicts, with the big difference that the poet, unlike that corrupted and corrupting force, offers us a glimpse of hope in a humanity not quite totally lost, not quite totally empty.

I read his poetry and feel exhausted, but not drained, exposed but not shamed, edified but not through false hope, enlightened but not tempted into orthodoxy - and always in awe of someone who knows his self and is willing to expose himself in the splendor of his nakedness.

As I understand his poetic purpose, he does not intend to hang the reader out to dry and closer to suicide (personal or collective), but rather as he honestly exhibits the emperor without clothes, you see a tender and loving heart that's beaconing us, warning us of the pitfalls, toils and snares we' have already come through, not only not to stumble with the same rock time and again, but to remove or at least clearly mark the obstacles for the benefit of the reader.

His poetry is, therefore, one of deep compassion and love.

— *Alfonso Maciel*

FlowerSong Press
McAllen, Texas 78501
Copyright © 2021 by Jeff Cannon

ISBN 978-1-953447-70-8
Library of Congress Control Number: 2021933497

Published by FlowerSong Press
in the United States of America.
www.flowersongpress.com

Set in Adobe Garamond Pro

Cover design by Matthew Revert
www.matthewrevert.com
Typeset by Elly Cridland
www.aeledapublishingservices.com

ANOTHER YEAR LIVING UNDER THE DRAGON STARS

Poems by Jeff Cannon

FLOWERSONG PRESS

Acknowledgements

Welcome reader! I hope you will enjoy and find some benefit from the poems in "Another Year Living Under the Dragon Stars". These poems cover love, race, growing up, life itself on the edge of looking up. Still seeing clouds and wondering where is heaven?

While questions linger, we always have poetry to rest on, gather and find ourselves once more. May these poems of almost a year be of some spirit value to you!!

I want to thank Lydia for always believing in my poetry, and for her ever- present support of my efforts.

Also, shout out to Jessica who graciously stepped in to help us both with a slight emergency. Thank you so much for your love and care. (The manuscript lived!)

I thank you Edward Vidaurre and Flower Song Press! Also bow graciously to your patience as I struggle with health issues to forge ahead and complete this effort which I have so whole-heartedly desired to do. No violins are playing, just the truth being spoken.

Each poem has its own grammatical flow regarding form, capitalization, etc. Titles are often the first line of the poem even though separated.

Health and Wellbeing to One and All,

Jeff Cannon

Table of Contents

A Brother Poet wrote - "Stay Blessed!"

Thx dear poet brother, i could use whatever blessings hard or soft
gentle or rough, sea breeze sweet, swamp dank like an old morning after
a long, too long of a night, a kindness from a bird flutter from above, a
bark but without teeth, or not too hungry snarl, there ain't much here to
chow down on now

That's why i got my thumb out on the corner, with the traffic or
the interested or not, the self-centered uncaring flotsam of my worst
dreams about the sharp suited killers, bank vault blood-letters or not

Cause it's mostly the not i find so clean and righteous smelly i almost
puke, no blessings come from them just spit, pistol pops that go through
me hot, so hot the wound sears up closed so i vanish in the crevice of a
sneeze, the blink of a poked eye, ouch, sore still sore from the mrs beatin'
on me since i did mess up, and she just broke down, a river raging angry
love, wanting still to bed me but finding it hard to swallow since i just
can't seem to hold up my end of the bargain

The one made where the roads crossed legs and closed their eyes, did
not want to see a damn thing nor feel anything like love since too much
pain, cracked too many windows and who has the grace to heal that
when i have no cash for even a half a tank of gas for what remains of these
feet, sore swollen misfits of time

So, by midnight you'll find me kneeling on the white lines at the far end
of the town, my hands up not in horror, or any hurry or any frenzy of
any other kind, just a patient, long suffering gesture for a blessing to
float my way

A soft kiss, affectionate, like the ones i want to remember, paint across
the basement of my mind, that company to keep me together, patched
up, my mouth shut so as not to spew something stupid at not a good time
to keep myself from being late for breakfast

Sure, wouldn't mind a blessing, if just a wave to stir the air to fill my
lungs, fan the flames of spirit to roar once more, lift me up, pick up one
foot and put it in front of the other, keep me upright and in motion to the
door today has open, and keep walking to the tune of the road unfolding
knowing i can keep on going, till the time my leather will slips leafy
from the dimming shades of my eyes

America Where Art Thou

On a porch rocking

A body from a Mississippi town dangling

Another Ferguson black man shot

before the White sun

A Latino barbed wire hung, a warning

A corporatist deal Las Vegas secret signed

Where congress and senate enjoy Bundt rallies

Nuremberg you are not dead

Your huge flags stamped with black wheeled time

Swirl still from Wotan's unholy eye

A blood waved sea yet feeds that imperial island

We wash ourselves in red guilt

Somehow smell better than bishops decked out in pink dresses

America Where Art Thou

From what balcony do you swoon as

your drones destroy for oil

your soldiers return in pieces

boxed up or shattered mind encased

America Where Art Thou

By the last drying water pool, tree, wolf, whale

bee hive, lark, lost child squeezed from the superior race

the last deal sealed with a dagger that needs to murder to feel

Adorable, holy, good

America Where Art Thou

i can't find you, if ever i could find

the real, you

A New Zealander jokes: "let's swap weather"; I answered

Or maybe a little something in between, you know kinda south
but not all the way down, where one slips into a puddle, just drains
away, beneath a raw sun, with an eye that won't quit, and a temper that
don't want to cool down, 'cause it just mean, mean as the desert stealing
everything out of your pockets, rippin' off your soul, and you wonder

What the hell was i born into, since no one spoke about the weather
when asked eyes would just turn kinda westward away, as if it was the
sunset's turn to answer, but the sun was tired, didn't want to hear a damn
thing, had enough for one day, just had that look that spoke, 'don't push me'

And what could a kid understand, being still so close to down
down felt like home, after those fights at school, the whippin's at home
down was already an intro to the heat that somehow would not give up
just, after a while, become part of your skin, like the heat wanted to
possess you, take you home with it, teach you about heat, let you feel a
real scorcher

Howl like the wolf, night critter hilltop lone, with his heat, and she was
heat but she was down, huh, down somewhere else, with a young buck
whose tail swaggered sexier than your shadow, so

You learned early the road you would be walking, down, while the sun
beat down, to remind you, you were not alone, you were being watched

so be careful or you might get burned and lose something important
until

One day came, the day with no name, except "Enough", and all the ages
of stories left your pockets, blew across fields, and your shadow thinned
out a mere shade of the you, you tried to keep from losin', but lost a
while ago, while down, and now down, feeling light, no longer heavy, no
longer hot, but cool just, holy cool, like heaven licked you

Hope it was, cause all the time under the sun, you deserved more than a
taste of heaven, for taking your sentence without complaint, just trying
every day to make the best of… down

Always the flip no matter how you are

How deep the cavern down in me, its surgical plunge into those landscapes of my heart, cleaves the unity of pulse into pieces of remembrances

Holy spaces keep what relics they can, safe, from the ravages of mind, flesh, fate, too vulnerable before the tumble of that gamble dice toss, that just once more, that ought not have seen the lust of night, since only you woke to sip what remained from my frozen lips

i did not experience horror only darkness, that bleak separation a robbery of every precious relic of a life, only the scent of you lingered to anoint me, finger paint your poetry over the places you most loved, so no one else would dare touch them, aware that trespass would damn them for eternity to encasement in stone

The penance for their sacrilegious taking of another's ground already claimed by love's blood, breast ripped tears, too many a lonely bed, chilled passion filling words into a verdict, justice into the sentence i deserved and laid across the altar of your fate

You delivered with leashed rage over my naked flesh a teaching against infidelity that only buries cherishment, leaves affection to survive on the dust of absence, live beneath the carnage of ruin, till what can heal from what solace endures, and what cannot, bleeds out the precious until no more can, and

Day and night dance together in the silence of a desire that sought more than a sip of pleasure, but that bone heat of bodies so, joined one becomes the other, the other one, without either losing their singular truth so quickly wrecked by this famished world from jealousy, so every kind of being suffers as much or more than it does, and we finally learn it's worthless to seek anything more than the aroma of your own freshly washed clothes

The heart does not know time, or need it really, it just beats

keeps it as it skips to the beat that makes it happy, regardless of

the weather or feel of day or night, up or down, that

uncomfortable squeeze of in between someone else's will

only the being there counts, wherever there is, since there

never lasts for-ever, possibly longer than one wants, but never

forever

in the never there is always a place to dance along and deeper

into, cause

the heart keeps the beat to the music, so the music plays, and so

can we, everyone not just children, even we the big serious

with pockets full of bills and worries

forget it

feel the beat, ride the pulse before one day it explodes elsewhere

into that beyond we have the freedom to paint anyway we want!

Be careful with your expectations

Just free to be, how simple, how wonderful, yet

how hard since so hard expectations encrust themselves to

bone, muscles, deep places where a fire used to burn so sweet

warm beautiful, connections make, without distinctions till

the cement poured and every act got filtered through the claws of

expectations

So many i could hardly stand up, yet did so because it was expected

i had to walk a certain way cause that was expected

sit, speak, stand, move in every way expected

execute every task, whether i was naturally made for it or not, as expected

Too small to argue, too scared of the consequences

i mean spanks hurt, and punishment was more painful since

shame got dumped over what was pure, just growing

free as a flower, tree, every other being except human beings

Those beings had to shed themselves to fit into every expectation

bury their fire, graveyard their very self, they got used to

finding in the mirror to fit it in as expected, or suffer dreadful consequences

as age made punishment worse, especially to become

an outcast, the alien with no group, no friends, an odd one, disassociated since,

that was expected of those different, odd, or simply defying expectations,

just being themselves, learning early to beg, borrow, steal, manipulate, hate, take power over, be in charge, so no one would ever punish them

again

Become priests, businessmen, politicians,

make laws weaved tight with more bitter expectations

make the deviant suffer execution for not exemplifying every expectation

push my hatred out on everyone, so i could feel good, very good

above all expectations

Finally, free of them, since no one could touch me anymore

i was no longer obliged by any expectations than to be

my anti-social, psychotic self

get revenge and bury all those who cursed me

made me to their image

constructed me into the freak marvel i am today

no longer a who, no longer a person, no longer a lover

living by the pulse of the heart

Be careful with your expectations

know where they come from, what they really mean

what they really intend to do, what they actually form, mold, manufacture

we arrived to be a human being related to others and the world

we share not

an alien, a monster produced by the unbearable inhuman furnace of

mighty expectations

Be well too, She said

i will be well as well as can be
i hope wellness is deep, dug by better hands than human
dug with better spirit than human
dug with better love than human
dug with poet, musician, artist… hands

though we try, we humans can't seem to escape some
bruise or battered wound to our souls
the kind that hurt too deep, too much, so wellness becomes
a puddle in a trashed road, still

i am years of healing though the ache, yet, when it rains
it will ...ache, still
i look up and thank the moreness for Her kindness i have felt
through all my seasons as i move into my 69th year of
growing up, finding out more about what it means to be a decent human
growing up and out of old bruised fingered grip

i dance into this day, joy fired, bliss glowing, grateful for
the wellness, i have to feel and feeling share at a second's notice!!

Blues Angel

Bluesy blouse of a look that says: "So what!"
Flapping from strung out corridors of lips
Scared elm of your body bends
In the cracked light of hallways
Stretched out like street cars
Parked in the belly of the dinner booth
The one with our names
Carved above the salt and pepper shakers

There i catch you falling out of the lap of night
Like a star into a pond of blue tears
Fingers of stray cats stretch across a wooden sea
Searching in the shadows of broken dreams
Splattered across the sunken face of the dead floor
For the halo you knew you came with

The one you put on last night
For sure
Before you left the musty flat of tapioca
The remains of soured corn flakes in a bowl
On the kitchen table

It was after you kicked
The underwear of memories under the bed

Blue not red
Not indigo
Only Blue

Like you my angel
The one i would find crying
By the window of my coffee
Spilling itself like my words
All over your dress

You poured cold water down the front of you
Suddenly you were no longer invisible

You emptied the dispenser of napkins to dab and scrub
Scrub and dab
While i held my coat open
To block the old men at the counter
From eating you with their watching
And losing their teeth

You dab heavy
Pounding heavy
Heating heavy
With a heat that never burned into a red
Only that fractured crystal of a blue
That kept you solid
Determined like a bird to keep its perch despite
All the crap coming down from the north

Across from the Gulf

Meeting like two freight trains on the same track

And crashing right over your head

To break the tender shell of your child

Into a snowstorm of feathers

Floating us both back to your blue home

Where we smoked blue cigarettes

And stripped off each other's blue clothes

To lick the blue coffee from each other's chest and fall

Into the treasure at the end

Of the smoky trail of inspirations

Drifting over everything

Painting everything

Changing nothing

Knowing time erased nothing

Only youth

Only muscle

Only movement

We stared out paned windows as the day returned

To sweep us back up into the blue flesh of our bodies

The bodies used but never taken

For what was taken always comes back

Nothing is ever lost

The body like the bed keeps everything in a blue chest

That just breathes and breathes and breathes

Blowing the dust of everything back

Covering our eyes with the cremains of night

The ashy spittle of day dries on our lips
So, our kisses like wooden matchsticks
Spark into a blaze of mad sulphur
Before coughing themselves back to sleep
The blue sleep that jumps on the licks of box cars
To ride the minor chords
That deliver us south
Back to the place of beginnings where
The tingling crescendo of notes descending
With each practical, earthy step
Stop
Jump off the edge of things and
Fall into a bucket of whaling E-flat
Always serving up that breakfast we've gotten used to
The battered sadness we can only eat
That smacks us out of thinking
Things could be any better with its
"Who the hell do you think you are?"

Oh, Blue Angel
Settle down, don't fuss
It ain't us that's sawing us apart
Settle down right here and settle the fuss
Right here with me by these tracks
Come on
Let's go home
i got two tickets in my pocket, Honey
So, Angel

You decide

We can't cut fate for certain

But this side of heaven, Angel

i know one thing for sure

We can fly together under the radar

Beat the cops

And out run the robbers too

Boardwalk early morning gift

What a wonderful gift to find on my Boardwalk, early mist
still ½ mast dawn eyes
light enough not to trip over shells of left-over dreams

Memories of drunk hop-scotch games played too old into night so
i arrived too late to my own shadow, find there left over mars bars
wrappers, remains of bark of squatting dogs, cats in bushes
still night damp immersed in their men's room morning drills

Oh, i turn a sloshed wave on bed beach low tide mellow
no sand in these britches, only the memory of morning alleluias, when
light brown hair sun combed, felt fun and fine and simply fabulous, with
some others of shared thoughts
for that exam we all would have gotten "A's"
passed that damned intro course to bull ****, meant to be a pain in our
ass, extra cash for the football coach

What frolic rises with Ocean City morning boardwalk salty fresh
every memory page blows in the breeze of waves exercising
their muscles, showing off for the guys, teasing the girls
looking for one last excitement with each other in the cool pajama parts
beneath the splintered walk called life
that spilt cool drink down your lap, just when it's your turn to sing

But with age like fine wine, you just groove to the guitar breeze playing the songs that made growing up easier, adulthood less a hard swallow of last week's gum finally falling from the roof of your mind

Bring me to the forest chapel

where you sing sweet melodies of your body safe

bear your soul so i can find mine

in each divine splash of that holy stream, where,

you bathe, preserve your truth

i want to feel your freedom run and laugh through my body

in that way become intimate in a way my mind cannot

experience

drench me with its subtle praises

scrub away in the loving way only you can do

with that purpose that would not hurt without

a cause, would discipline only to bring me closer to

the moreness your forest and its waters allow

to flourish, call me to know, become that wisdom

after having your tender hands scrub away my white histories

your kind massage, steady me with its hard press

unclog the stalled traffic in me, called… lies

Clear from my eyes the ads of billboards, tv, radio

uncover those hidden in the pigment of every

painting, print of every book that somehow excludes

the breath of your flesh, the presence of your soul, so

i will come closer to you and by doing so

come closer to knowing myself a little more real than

i accepted… yesterday

"Bumble" she whispered

Her eyes an ocean pre-dawn mood, stare between
starless thoughts, unsure of what to do, if what will make a
difference or, if the "do" would do any good, since a left hand
index finger just made it to the board, the place a bee stuck in
the bull's eye, can no longer be "bout" its "bumble"

All's stuck between the skull eyes, staring diamond through
purple curtains, stiff from silence, blind to seeing anything but
everything they want, while wishes sit on foreheads huddled
frightened, beneath dark sun glass plastic tents, waiting, just
waiting for some sunny news, but all the mailman brings is rain

The only one getting fatter, the humidity that steals the water
every landscape turns stiff cardboard, not a breath disturbs the
dead, for living even as long as they did, they have earned
undisturbed eternal sleep, the peaceful, no longer aggravated
ulcerated, mean, frustrated, skeleton figments of anguished
hope, sold at the market for less than a poor person's 1/4 of a
day's pay, or a bologna day old sandwich on the black market
that lucky yesterday, when the earth shook a San Francisco tilt
and good luck fell from the sky my way

As soon as i sighed happy, felt 20 knives splice through my
shirtless flesh, what remained of me fell soulless, all over the

Senate floor, where everyone was screaming, no one hearing or
wanting to hear, just getting off on the circle jerk, as one
collapsed flaccid, another jumped in to fill the place, no need for
votes, they no longer count, corporate cash has every spot held
in velvet bondage

The luckless maiden just sits and stares, she dare not even flinch
a sneeze will alert a sniper, she'll be done for instantly, so she
the witness of the slobber, insanity, every teardrop from some
reckless cruel, can never tell, only store in rooms filling up with
centuries of blood-soaked crimes, unfinished chapters of
decapitated heads, ash bookmarks of pillage, rape torched
evidence, mountain cave smoked so the guilty remain innocent
the innocent just voiceless numbers of psychotic bookies
fingering, ibm punch card keyboards, hidden deep beneath
every capital of every so-called free nation, so

The maiden eyes of predawn mood, stare between starless
thoughts, she can't move, she's become the rock of ages, the
testimony of what happened to the Caucasoid empire of fools

Should any interstellar traveler unluckily stumble upon, this
cancerous mound of nothing more than encrusted ego goo
shock her from her 1/2 dream life by the question: "what
happened here?"
would only scare her not 1/2 way but all the way to death!

"But Thursday is too far"

The far, that kind of away, outside time, sticking its tongue out
at space, duties, limitations of any kind

The far away, enough to once more misplace the golden slippers
an angel gave sometime after midnight, in the seam of
moonless silence, the place nothing stirred, not even the bony
memory of last year

Simply it clanked in the wind, the way fresh cut bamboo strung
together does, spanked by those breezes with such hard palms
the kind that all too soon leave the mark of their presence, as if
they knew you needed something to remember, something to
bring with you into the next yawning day

Something to know, yet must that something always sting, ache
when you walk, sit down for a break from the pilgrimage that
leads nowhere except, the sandy beach of child's play and that

laughter, stolen from you by the palms, stuffed into your mind
already crammed with too many chores, detailed tasks
obligations that when done leave you, standing alone on the
porch hungry, so

You can't remember the golden slippers, the ones you drew and colored in as a child, even stayed within the lines, but no one

applauded you, they just yelled, "What are you doing?

Get in here and wash up!! It's time for dinner!!

It was always time for dinner, just when dreams began to dance

joy smiled over us in the yard, despite our calloused toes, the

salty sweat in our eyes

My eyes caught yours, for a moment something pleasant tingled

in our bodies, we got close, but you got scared and ran into

your house, and i ran into mine for fear as well

Still, despite the far, i can remember that pleasant something so

close, yet ripped far away, as a way as these gray eyes on this

worn porch trying not to remember too much, since too much

brings tears
the rains of having missed watching you dance for me in those

golden slippers...

Circles play their color while

your face turns shades of thoughts
mellow eyes flip damp pages, cosmic sighs
spill their unlaced histories of all their tears
across my bare landing strip chest

The holy station waiting for arrivals whole or in part
whatever, i have time now to lay back, simply spin
without worry since, i have finally learned of course by
the uncomfortably prickly side-way, that all the rushing will not

Move the traffic, only stain the vibrant orbits of majestic blues n greens
those orange suggestions tingle laced with darling purple haze to charm
the pants off any puritan, make every evangelical a… sinner, every
lutheran have to sing another hymn with 50 verses, every catholic to
kneel until the priest finds the right key to unlock the confessional, while

Memory throbs me to scream "do it again sweet olive girl!"
maybe this time the window-pain will shatter, free those captured
in purgatory to cheer and merrily dance the seasons round, bless
with rose petals, the grandmother sinking slowly back to her serenity
restorative… bed
while you with your hunger already satisfied with dandelions
blossom magnificent on the simplicity of my belly

We laugh, spin all the colors dizzy with the laughter we thought we
forgot, but now recall from the dungeon of forgotten, so
every ring of splendor fits your eye's desire
my flesh-boned bark, paw claw tapping to splash into that longing
that…

First, embarrassed thrill so tingling everything got anointed moist that
night, that first of celebration nights when body press births delight
frees wonder to wash the world of pain, our life from the anguish of our
loneliness come dusk, when colors collapse into dim corners, radiance
drops spent ashes, what's left sits next to us a loyal pet, while we finally
again, resign ourselves to do our homework and… persevere to possibly
this time… get it right!

Dog-sled message through
the storm here swirling snow

i have not turned into a grump
it's just that i have a number of projects i need to complete
labors that in their own way are soul works

They urge me to attend to them.
my bones ache from their tears when i neglect them
to pay bills, try to rub a nickel from two pennies
like most of us

Accept the heavy winter releasing stored up gusto this year
to chill and cover us constantly with its dusty mayhem

Find comfort in the old ways that explode penny crackers now leave more
ashes to wake up to
briefer moments of relief from the strife of feeling
that un-sheeted, naked circumstance that provides no protection between
myself and the pain of tyranny, the horror of suffering here and around
this world for such insane, obnoxious reasons

Words land in pieces when the muse arrives
older than tomorrow, uncombed
splashed with torn residues from where she has had to sleep
skeleton thin, she collapses, rests on my shoulder, silent

while the moon herself walks slowly barefoot

sad faced from the soreness her eyes cannot hide from her awareness

Beauty huddles cold on street corners

goodness bent old before its time, toothless, ambles

unable to speak the truth still pulsing through weary veins

a candle worn down, almost snuffed out from the mad traffic racing to

find the prize buried in the lie branded into their weeping skin

its tears cover their petroleum tracks

Slight anointing for tiny creatures extinguished in the great death rush of

our age

the times our children drink from

learn from, rush to us with pride

seek from our arms a warm embrace for their thin accomplishments

our kiss to bless what they take as success

the triumphs of hard work that fill the now with glory

but only postpone the real gift of tomorrow

Earth home vitality, life zest for community among her people

love gift ever caring

hospitality's opened door despite

the darkness devouring everything

while promised affection gets exchanged into profit

shoveled into already stuffed pockets far away

gated away in stern mausoleums of putrid grandiosity

Do You Really Know

both sides of the clouds, the clump of earth in your hand
the screams of someone getting a beating
pillowed tears of lonely caress
the toll that calls the life to depart the body, put aside the
struggle about, with, for the things of this world, only to contend
with what exists on the other side

To know both sides or at least something, of each is
to embrace the semen and the egg, those energies when bonded
birth endurance, bound by strong fibers that grip bone to flesh
heart to muscle, mind to breath, so each day becomes less scary

Only another replay of some yesterday, blowing across the
landscape of your chest, that vast oasis of treasures waiting for
your fingers to make love with them, your stripped down
existence to finally enter the realm of their naked knowledge
let it be a holy oil to anoint you into another day of better
navigating simply, being alive...

Doves Otherworldly

arrive mystical radiant, rainbow feathered fanned
their angelic beaks, brilliant, dip peacefully into infinity
dark luscious empty, yet so full, crowded with precious
yet, still so accommodating

An epiphany of elegance they balance on the breath of an
ancient prayer, still moist from those archaic lips still
marked by love, if one has the eyes, the thought, the
time to more than glance, but stop to gaze at what calls
so softly with the slight tug of a child for company, before

The physicality of what was more than memory loses flesh
from the hungry squander of the day about to unleash its
growling deities tugging at the circumference of awareness
about to break loose for the freedom to devour, join
the flaming madness of traffic faces speeding into their
somewhere, their some want without seeing, leaving only a
cloud of ambition's dusty nothingness

Clueless to the cause of children without school lunches
freedom for forest people, release for those corralled in horror
chambers along the border of frenzy to create history, while
the homeless are plowed into garbage cans, wake up floating

with the plastic animating the pacific seas, while others become
red-lined into broken buildings without affection, only the
music, scratchy murmurs of tomorrow, that sound the same as
yesterday with

One's mind a thread of please, held between thumb and fore-
finger, the place where doves otherworldly, flutter, offer the
food of sacred epiphanies that drip from their holy beaks

Ever able, ever present to feed the humble real, those still honest
unable to prostitute themselves, those who still cherish fidelity
for every kind of 'other' starved in an unholy world of raped
mystery guarded by guns held by too many, too eager trigger-
happy fingers

Dragon Stars

dragon stars shine, just watch out for their spit

their juice falls invisible, not like the shower of a shooting star

they don't make waves if not a party for themselves

they sacrifice nothing, everything belongs to them

none is to be shared, only legally refurbished so,

the dragons keep a style they believe they were born to possess

the style that dominates, keeps holy their tabernacle selves

no one else, just they can touch, but when the lights are out

watch out: things get more raw in the dark

dragons have quite the 'rep', everyone looks up to them

so precious, yet so far removed

just a slight breeze from their passing by

feels a grand pat on the head, something good for the 'us' who

toil, obey, offer our lives to die for dragon liberty to claim whatever

they deem to supply more coin to fill the lining of their elephant pants

we, below, continue despite the propaganda about the red, white, true

blue, while others scale every barrier set up to keep us fighting over

who gets a chance to swing on the 'public' playground swings

aware that respect for those who look, feel, wish, hope, toil in good faith

keep the front porch an always gathering place to pick off fleas, cut hair, simply talk square about the unfair, daily falling from the imperial sky

as if there was no way to outfox an unnecessary concocted curse

time will dispatch the arrogant ones dressed in the treads of their crimes

the dragon stars can spit all they want, one day

they'll find themselves in the oil of their heinous deeds…frying

Each one we meet

unravels an untouched, unfelt thread of flesh
finds for us another connection to relationship not just more
worried traffic, belly clenched bleeding, nervous tension
lunchroom separations, polite but empty conversation

too many threads have been lost, plucked out, to get ahead on a
bicycle for only one to pedal on a road with sweaty others
zigzagging to cut off each other, crash fear about too much
competition, so the robust metallic machine i am becoming will
have all that is to have, preserve the mortgaged hut and yard i
claim as mine, when it is owned by so many fat others
frothing at the mouth to leap on it with the first late payment

ahhhh... that more threads of human sensation, heart pulse
spirit commonality could surface from the arctic ice of
ego thrust, mind eye dark plastic focused

ah to find the thread that opens me up to the all, the moreness
wonder, the waiting precious to be embraced not raped and
slaughtered, not sentenced to burn at the pyre of righteous
religious applause, not languish bleeding in already drenched
streets of black, brown, immigrant bodies just wanting to be
to be their human selves, to be the freedom that sings through
their veins

and i too, released from the prison of superiority

liberated to be as well part of the precious

no longer the predictable obedient, thoughtlessly unreflective

out of touch with the vile willfulness of vicious robbers of

precious Life!

Be well as always, my wish

Despite

The weather that dropped your pancake day

exploded your sarsaparilla night all over everything important

the morning that decides to sleep in and doesn't let you know, so

the toast burns, the buses run laughing from your frantic waving hands

never mind your shoes are ruined, your new dress is dreadfully stained

Do not worry

it is all in the deck of neatly shuffled cards

they will change

wait on the street corner of soft breathe, untangled hair

sit on the bench waiting for you

relax there, its shaved slats will hold you, comfort your back

embrace your cheeks with soft palms, cross or uncross your legs

there is nothing to get crucified about

simply be, watch with hand in hand resting a tiny bird almost

featherless from searching so hard for home, being so good, you

have ulcers to prove it, a list of everything given up for

love, for penance, for looks, sex, bed and breakfast

an occupation not just a blow job, recognition of a life with flesh

significance as itself without having to prove anything to make it worthy

Sit on that bench waiting for you, find yourself there, know again your

name from head to toe, like the first time you discovered yourself and smiled

Edward!!

As no life could ever keep you, no prison will ever hold you
that poetry pulse is the only leash, if that to keep you rooted in
one spot long enough to father those verses that will knit
together another child, your child

your flesh and blood child that incarnates all the history, secrets
celebrations, pain, tears, laughter, grudges, lost jobs, all the
many little and large jobs, a few blow jobs to fill lonely spaces

refresh time, downshift into the next deal, that dice toss to
rewrite fate, or try at least to make it sound better, even though
the feel don't change, nor the memory, Picasso etched, in some
rear room of mind that elastic place sometimes a prison
sometimes a landscape wide open, so wild you just roll for days
in the fragrance of poetry that just sweats out of you, makes you
hungry

starved for a mic even if just a few drunks are in the shadows
snoring through your best lines, while a few chicas giggle
wiggle their goodies to catch your eye, hook your lips to
stop sounding and start licking the garden where the jewel
swells, ready for you

the way those multiple word pictures drip leave you in a

semi-coma, the only delight worth fighting for, never sleeping
just fever working through night street lamp hours to fashion
that flesh that offers itself without a word to make words better

fit your tongue, the cadence of your breathe, the pulse of
your presence, bolder than the axis, where love pants its prize
for you and no place, no time can wrestle you down, keep you
locked in one where it is or was, or never wanted to be

just on the open plain where the winds kissed your naked
offerings
that silence after the last word shut the door on that baby that
grew up fast, faster than a brush fire, a real scorcher to land you
a 'visiting poet's' post at the university you always wanted to go
but never had the grades in those yesterdays, but in this now
have the cohunes to howl through every barrier and praise the
day you were born, and everything wanted or not that came to
you to make you who you are and more...!!

Elderhood

the way sometimes elderhood feels, the sense that all's been done
nothing's left but dreams that float as colored helium, hot air now
the way breath wheezes from strained lungs, tired of the same old job
like the bowels and my man, always having to wake up thinking about
what he's supposed to do, then keep me waiting, almost so to fall asleep
standing a weary statue no longer on solid ground, waiting for a mighty
gusto or just a sneeze to topple me, crash me and all of what's kept
in my bones, so many stories walking the same fields as all those
yesterdays
their soil blown nowhere, no use, it makes no sense to the youth
constantly changing trains, one faster than the other, to keep up the
speed, reach that of lightning, so there is no pondering, wisdom, real
knowing for sense would be made, the crooks revealed for who and what
they are, democracy as shame, just the rich making and changing "laws"
for themselves, not us, just keep us stupid enough to do their bidding
take their crumbs and say: "thank you"!
well so much for this, i'll take the silence, accept the wind erasing me
my voice, my footprints, and shadow, i had my shot and took it
had my fun, enjoyed it, no need for tears, just a light suitcase for
traveling, one that won't herniate me, that's all i need, enough has
postponed my trip to the great beyond, enough's enough, i feel good
 today, maybe i can catch a ride on a balloon

Every time i exhale

The image of you walking through the light door towards my night body
sleeping, water well bucket deep, tangled up in cemetery webbed graves
once so neatly set in black and white rows, as if life and its worlds could
ever be so neat and trustworthy

Thoughts colored according to the horror or delight set off by those
domestic kitchen wars where broken plates lay beside broken heads
where blood replaced catsup on the triple-burnt-to-death hamburgers
those bar booth 'get backs" where fancy drinks got slapped into each
other's faces, cops had to come pry us from each other's throats with
electric fingers

Every time i exhale the fury sounds less harsh, the scenes less vivid
the colors less stark, i, more free, navigate a midnight ceiling no longer
starry blood splashed, cursed hurled favorites no longer echo off
my headboard

Only the sound of lost traffic spills through the window, with another
new shade, i feel sorry for it, neither window nor frame has had the
ovaries to disturb its delight of finally being in a home
they figure the shade will find out sooner or later what life is like living
on this planet, in this ego scorched realm of killing prayers and hate
litanies, organ draped music over incensed coffins of street corner white-
christened dreams, but it was no freudian penis or jungian vagina held in

hand, just a plastic cell phone with a ring call sounding "Bang! Bang!"
Every time i exhale my sight gets clearer, i discover more of what i was
never told, since silence had its tongue nailed to the floor of its mouth
i grew-up-in the cocktail bowl of swirled winds, the way stocking feet
sound walk ever so slightly over a plush golden living room rug, so

i drifted toward those stacks of green, red, yellow, purple books, they
helped some, but were always hazy on the details, especially when it
came to the darker stuff, like 'the truth", how swift a leap back into the
light, that whiteness be honored at all costs, (for the sake of one's tenure)
there is no real color line, fool! it's a wealth line, but i digress-

i was too scared to dig, feelings were hard to decipher, i felt safer in my
head, had a lot of junk to memorize, make the grade, get ahead, i let
music rock my feelings roll my moods, i just hit repeat so my head-
phones blasted "This could be the Last Time" or later, "White Room"

Every time i exhale now, the figure changing faces ever haunting me crumbles more away, it's absence allows a peaceful presence, soft affection, a welcome benevolence warms me from inside out, forms a safe abode wherein i find the quietude of my body, wanting to find me hold me, let me become more intimate with the rings of its bones, the songs of its flesh, the stories pulsed through veins to cleanse blood rivers, plow clear choked airways of what was but now is not, to not waste what's precious now, heal ancient wounds, to be more humane for others, self, this world

Every time i exhale, sometimes i find another's honest fit, bone true presence to feel and give, celebrate being vibrant present, finish each other's sentences, not to stifle from ego control, jealousy or fear, or insecure power possession, rather from body awareness, non-verbal link of sensual knowing, artists of humane living, gifting till our tired flesh seeks nothing more than to curl up in blessed rest

In the arms of final moments, realize we were never just hot air exhaled and forgotten, but ever a gift, despite the rough spots still so loved and so worthy to be cherished!

Flakes of precious body

Sail broken vessels smashed dream packed
across a bloody sea stripped of beauty
without any affectionate memory

Blue life tries to fly, escape the sentence of the menace
that never sleeps, but ever awake, lays ready to pounce
on those unaware, steal what is most precious and leave
them abandoned to fend for themselves

Others fare differently since their temperament is too kind
too human, so their bodies dissolve, quickly, possibly mercifully
into the depths of silence

Still memory hides in the forest of sharp knives, while eyes still search
through blinds that offer some protection from all declensions of harsh
nonacceptance, the pestilence of shame, the inhumanity of forced labor
where only one's death makes the industry of living happier since
another fresh, young, new lifer can work faster and cost less

Regardless, fresh body wounds of now still bleed from stripes of
yesterday, the bruisers lining up to fill tomorrow fight each other for
space of head, neck, back, shoulder to colonize what's left untouched by

the arrogance of torment

No medicine exists to heal the body heart, soul spirit, bone of those grandiose mad lizards of dominion leashed together, a family of one faith that offers forgiveness for the crimes of rabid hearts that want more at any price, since they will be escalated to heaven and enjoy the blessed banquet of their god

While we don't count, until we spit out the lies of separations force fed us since our birth, bury them, embrace each other as relatives of our bone and flesh, march arm in arm, embraced together, a huge wave of true humanness before the killing darkness

Our loyalty of shared sacrifice and love will seal the pledge of revolt keep us honest and do only what is needed since enough death has marked the earth, scarred our conscience

A life force thrives within us, not a religion, class, philosophy or politic to unite us, to remember the cry of each other, the shared space of our bodies, the faces of each other, the suffering of each of our bodies every concept of power erases from mind and conscience

The room enough for the us of the future to rewrite the fate now polluting ourselves and our home, since we are incarnations of goodness, the promise of life repair, the possibility of communion, the truth of communal respect

Task sharers for the larger good that allows everyone what they need and more, the cherishment of embracement to deeply feel and never forget we are loved for simply being here, recognized not as something special but necessary bearers of gifts, remain humble, honest, able to ensure spirit-heart prosperity, the fullness of life, not certain pockets with bloody currency

The celebration of a human death through which one joins the loving memory of brave and gifting ancestors whose memories become a spirit food to nourish humane and earthly life…

For Certain

You stand sure, so self-possessed, owner-Gardner
guardian of your presence from head to toe, front to back

Your sharp eyes, MRI scan deep, to know if his
outside story matches the one you hear grinding within
you brook no nonsense, and if he flubs up that's it
no time for fibbers, growing liars, maturing players of some
high sidewalk set, out for a game of nighttime sweaty plunder
no phone numbers, once is enough, it's onto the next hottie!

But you know from experience, the only thing elastic is
the pain, and one slip was and is enough, you got the lesson
still feel it now, a kind of protection memory, reality check
a re-con-sid-er of your take on the present slick talk, hip cloth
suave moves, so cock sure, but, "he goona loooooose his head if
he come too close!" yep! an alarm sounds "he stinks of the past"

i hear your inside talk about: "the past i'll never let be present again,
once was enough, i still have a mark, yeh, he left a mark as if to brand
me make me part of his corral, i'm not hard just aware, i'm not
jaundiced just knowing what needs to be known, so nobody,
no-b-o-d-y dare has a thought to even for a moment think of

taking possession of ME! i own Me and no one else ever will!!"
"Only the one who wants to be With me, share the day like a
lunch sandwich, be together as one, side by side, weaved
together as one breath, one pulse, one thought burning for the
other not just the pleasure of or for one's self, ah! ah!! Ah! AH!
AHHH!!! "You hear me? You understand me?"

"This face don't lie! i will be the gift person you ever met in this
world and would sacrifice and die for, or your 'worst enemy 'as
the saying goes... So, what will it be? Your call! i don't have all day!"
i smile relieved, knowing for certain, you'll be o-k!!

For you Dear Presence, Deep Poet,
Devoted Bearer of Soul Sacred
Art

Flower garden body precious, keeps sacred stories safe

histories with all their dent's and hues of holiness flourish where

landscaped chapels shelter every courage forged artistic monument

Your resilient flesh keeps every treasure of your dearness strong for

confrontation or healing through passion drenched verses, so we learn to

know and more so feel the way to navigate the inconsistent weather of

this world, persevere in solitude or solidarity

Keep heartfulness where it belongs, so lips speak uninhibited lessons of

histories to uplift, partake of body testament not just fluff of pedestrian

tales that when swallowed evaporate, leave us ignorant despite every

stuffed shirt we might wear to appear so much better than our

neighbor, when the pants we wear too tight bust their seams, expose our

dumb, bare ass

That i could be as fearless as you, take up the needed labor of perpetual

self-discovery, daily liberate the more that waits for freedom

incarnate the simple truth of our only real labor, to extend our arms to

welcome, our palms to bless the other who complements the marrow of

our spirit, the morning pulse of our holy blood, affection's vow to keep

each other a sacred garden, an Eden good enough

cared for by precious artworks of presences in process

Fruit fell

in my lap as the dew of waking dawn, squint of light not yet awake
the angle of the bark my dog shoots at me, impatient at my lateness
how dare i sleep in when he has to be let out, free himself
leap in his freedom, feel the delight of his animal nature
the way i want to feel delight guarded in my bones

Coursing through my veins, cleansed by my heart, blessed by my spirit
almost as gray as me, yet younger than eternity still, that mystery moves
me without complaint

i hear no words floating ill will on the ocean wind
the smell of fresh city greets me, washes me in the manners and mood of
human grit already warm from the heat of tires and temper, cutting the
day with curses, to relieve oneself, as if dark words would paint
anything different
than bleakness
do they really relieve one of that pressure slept on all night, unrelieved
needing release but find no arms open enough, breasts liberated enough
body less damaged than the fists of night, neglect of day

What solace greets this morning when the same song plays
the grandmother in the window prays, the father swings punches, as if
to clear the drunk leftover from last night, leaves black eyes in his wake
his oldest already turned into a hit man, prepares to avenge the pain

clear the path to heaven for the rest of his family by his sacrifice since
he believes he will one day be the savior of his family like jesus is
proclaimed as savior of mankind by his death and rising like the sun

Pobre muchacho, he believed the nuns spoke the truth, and the young
priest could stand in and be his father, as i did want when i was not gray
possessed by stroke and left in another city to live out the sentence of
my days, watch and pray for something different, the different that
had no chance, the right rain never came to water hearts the way each
needed to flourish

Heart praise

For the ones whose pulse orbits out beyond mind fences that
encase one in concerns about their own backyard

For the ones who bleed for truth, seal the honesty of
eyes and tongues so only the real as real can be despite
the unreal of the all around us

Heart Praise
For the ones who anoint touch with sacrifice, so, less wounds
pierce another's sacred flesh, keep that temple holy, undefiled

For the ones who feel and feeling keep safe erotic beauty
hold dear sensual explosions so no one gets hurt
leash the urge to conquer, the need to abuse
see the other another self, struggling to be seen as precious
not a thing, a trophy, hot street corner topic, barroom headline

Heart Praise
For those who relish life, make each day a gift to Let the other
feel worthy to be, just for being

Heart Praise
For those who incarnate the recognition of affection
tap Life waters to wash away the burden of shame, heal

scars of neglect, undeserved punishment, the ultimate abandonment

Heart Praise

For those who realize Valentine's day has nothing to do with
arrows, candy, silly cards that only strip love to an advertisement
cheap mockery of what gracious living is really about despite the
dollar signs on every, person, living presence that twists them into
another commodity of unleashed appetite

Heart Praise

For every Heart that pulses to Love, knowing more than we could ever
know or want to know about ourselves and has not chosen to give up
on us, erase us but embrace us, love us until we get it and can love
ourselves and others more!

Home

HOME?... WHERE HOME?... WHAT HOME?... the HOME
now, the now full of cruelty, the blood to prove it, a broken
water faucet slow painful drip down, trembling wall

The wall that doesn't forget, can't forget, centuries of agony
waves still rumble through it, still a witness to that unnecessary
ego release of pain, compensation for wounded pride, mistakes
made and caught and publicly called out for making

Shame draped over shame, soul corrosion hungry, eating away
every minute, every shred of self-worth, the shame weaved into
curtains, slammed door thunder shaking house, bodies…
lightening shouts of venomous rage, that home of swollen eyes
frightened face, slamming shut then open with every breathe
every want for escape, every want for revenge to end the horror
plague, the one that leaves too late, returns too soon, those steps
that auger ill, sweep up fast the little one to curl up inside in the
tent of my ribs for shelter

The last place i always found to fit, make it to dawn and the next
as pages of days flipped over and over again until the movement
of their knowing brought me to this place, the next one of all
those promised peaceful next ones, this time the breeze quiets…

Is this the destination of my nomadic life, the end of the
temporary drill, that unpacks so much, not everything just yet, we
have to see, we have to see…

i do not hear that woeful litany, maybe, just maybe, this place is
the place i rest, settle down and into, make a home not just a
tent, my lined face and weary bones do so mightily hope this
place is, the fulfillment of my days

"How am I?" I pondered, then replied:

In between the lavender feel of 4 am coffee and the heavy quilted
disclosures of your weeping breasts wanting my tongue to soothe your
nippled loneliness beneath the wool blanketed subway platform of your
bed

Marked by all the sights and sounds, wants and illusions, shamed spit
back, holier than thou walk by, all the hard and grabby as if you were a
piece of fruit at a market stand, not a woman being, glorious in your own
standing, precious through your showing up the way you do, to mix it up

Yes, toss in the laughter and those ass pats to shake out the too serious
flip the shoulder chip far away from the horizon of your thought, free
your eyes to see the other side of everything to better weigh, the con-
sequences of good and not so good, find the best hidden in the stuffed
rack of better, avoid a painful sentence of too many days

Locked away from the usual, the loss of the casual, no more close only
distance of cold bars and striped pajamas, black slippers and those
damn too big panties, that keep slipping from your ass crack no matter
how hard you clench your sweet cheeks to hold on to a wad of material,
keep those damn panties up along with your pride, yep
All this and the more that sighs from your inviting lips to remind me of
the prize at the bottom of the cereal box, and remember that other colors
remain left over from my night dreams

"The day won't be that dark, baby," you whisper, the child in me jumps in your arms to hold hard that teddy bear faith, keep close that something… to hold despite, the silence of the forest, the restless curses of street painting sidewalks with no other meaning than chipped pieces of their fancy spray-painted dreams momentarily passing by, as if they were the one and only… truth

I am falling down

Hug me baby, hug me baby, hug me tight, cause i am falling down
hug me baby, oh my baby, hold me tight
nothing's underneath me, just a fresh dug grave

Hold me baby, hold me baby, oh hold me with all your heart
save me from the reaper's cut
hold me baby, hold me baby, oh hold me with all your heart
save me from fate's will for this poor boy

Hold me baby with your sweat and bones, hold me baby with all your
sweat and bones, a mad wind's blowing
hold be baby with your sweat and bones, hold me baby with all your
sweat and bones, dark clouds hunting me
their sharp fingers clawing after me

Ain't nothing most folks can do, if standing alone, fate's too swift
if you ain't got someone on your side, pleading your cause before
the almighty, nothing one alone can do

Hold me baby, hold me baby, oh hold with all your heart
save me from the reaper's cut
hold me baby, hold me baby, oh hold me with all your heart
save me from fate's will for this poor boy

Hold me baby with your sweat and bones, hold me baby with all your
sweat and bones, a mad wind's blowing
hold be baby with your sweat and bones, hold me baby with all your
sweat and bones, dark clouds hunting me
hear their claws against the cobble stones

Sure, as i am pleading, i know you won't let me fall, no baby
now you just hold me tight, love me with your soul, yeah baby, that's
right, that's right baby, cause i'm doing the same for you

We'll hold each other, oh we'll hold each other
if fate takes one, he gonna find his pockets full
and he won't be going anywhere
we'll hold each other, oh we'll hold each other
if fate takes one, "he gonna find his pockets not so full"
a voice whispered in my ear

I am

love's night heat moist remains settled now
a cool dew across the front lawn of your mind
awakened sweetly by the gentle massage of
morning's soft warm palms

the hope you will notice my prayer of supplication
from your compassion filled pocket
leave me a cup of cool water
resurrect me from the incarceration of a child left unnoticed

faith's ointment of ages, tender blessing for every page of
your wisdom book, sheltered in the tabernacle of your
heart fed care

the answer to untie the silence that binds your waist
the word to liberate your day to share with you the
abundance of its lavender blessings

I am lonely in the face of death

i am lonely in the face of death

darkness smiling without a sound

only the thump of my pulse to nail my body

together, or try to persist in the attempt to keep something real

as real as something together can be, after all that

other hammering, years of tearing down, putting back up

all the paint overs did nothing but obscure the truth

did not make it real, only a gaudy roadside show

yes, i am lonely in the face of death

the way i was at Palisades Amusement Park or

my second-grade desk, or gas pump at the out island

the one closest to the street where all the action

actioned, all right, into another dust of 4th of July display

all those fiery paper lies finally landed to show themselves

empty, empty, empty as myself in body suddenly feeling gutted

wondering what it lived for, what life did want to live for

after all the sacrificial changes due to the weather of acceptance

when worth packed up with another name, journeyed to another

'promise' place that, like time, wound down to show itself, leave me

empty before every responsibility that cried outside my front door

hungry to be fed, as hungry as the dark for the truth of my shadow

words of scotch-taped wishes, eloquent lifts from another's ancient speech that cost lives then and still now

there's something about forever, it never changes despite

the thump of my pulse now pulsing for its own sake, for the only act it

knows how to do, was born to do the only urge left to believe, that

darkness and silence like meanness and killing, like death is

only a dim landing meant to be scary, meant to wake us up

meant for a miracle, not a birthday candle to be blown out, to be real

at the end of all the testing, still push lonely against that dark

step lonely still across that threshold, since no one else can move

what remains of you or me, still find courage to hold onto when

my fingers search my dusty pockets,

find

after crossing, acceptance by the real and true

waiting for company

I can speak or...

just sit there beside you, and pass the Oreos if you just need
another presence to keep you grounded on another day's subway
ride through 'same ol city blues'...

When the colors melt into your trousers leave a stain that won't
come out, just another lousy that makes one wonder, "i just got
up and on time, what did i do wrong, already?" and the 'already'
feels too late and the late paints everyone in gray suits

See the key word here is paints, just throw some more water on
your face, cool, cold, colder water, wake up blessed water

Deeper water, for a more grateful wake up, turns a miraculous
high power garden hose its splash washes away the paint, scrubs
stains gone, resets the station to the heart music flowing
"oh, Yeah" in your veins

Your lovely waiting in the kitchen for a powerhouse "Oh Baby"
 and your "ol' boy" perks up, happy to oblige, the sun bursts its
freedom, i walk a smile into the light, leave the Oreos behind!

I cannot tell

if the table is or i am the reality trembling
at the edge of the crumbling path

i thought i had gotten over being scared of the world
so foreign, so cruel, so unapproachable so unknowable
but
when the fresco peeled away from the wall, memory
waved good-by in pieces on the floor too tiny for
my trembling fingers to pick up

the pieces so small the way stars paint me across the
shrinking universe behind my eyes where suddenly
peace can thrive, satisfaction blossom, pleasure now
free explode its delight
that glorious relief of age, time turned kind leaves for last
to rob from the flesh

my palms, now crease- dried replicas of my sovereignty, once
translators of the language of touch, grow small, withdraw
from the world without a memory, since the fresco peeled away

my eyes too gone to see, pull down their shades
my dreams no longer know their home
it no longer stands where they have run

the wind has swallowed the address

the sun no longer keeps its hours, the moon

no longer dances to make night tingle

all is incense and myrrh wrapped in silence

just tight enough to feel safe, sigh and let

everything, dissolve into the air

safe, there is no need for soundness just the safety

of being gently handled finally so relaxed and

more alive than all the years that only stole goodness

left in its place unwanted surprises that made no sense only

aggravation

the only medium now, liquid silence, buoyant

frankincense kisses unleash every binding, bill, sub-

mission, free the i once jailed in my false name

imprisoned in a place of combat despite all the talk of

otherwise

all the scented love cards

the true of me, sails free without concerns

since the fresco peeled away from the wall to leave

just the sweet songs of stars, caress of soft jasmine

the warm bosom of safety to curl up into… finally

I missed you

My kisses will be wet with anguish
loneliness born from the waiting space occupied by
one when enough room is prepared for two, since
i in my foolishness wandered thoughtless to look back
check if, your lantern shown through the early morning darkness

My stumbling tiredness got the better of me, stuffed my gray
wits in its pocket as if to play a trick, there is no fault to punish
no meanness smirked across the horizon to sting me, only
silence lifted me from the hardness

Silence kind enough to deliver your message, the slight
check mark in the sand, to let me know you had passed by
stopped to let me know you remembered me as the day called
you into the slow boiling frenzy of your obligations, already
barking at you, nipping at your heels as you moved a slight
gazelle into the routines of the day that beckon for you to
comfort it with your presence

Make it feel safe to keep walking, bring the sun with all his
tricks, gifts, obligations, presents, pain and, goodness to spill
upon the cautious and reckless, the humble and proud, those
awake and those only 1/2 conscious fumbling around with their
usual excuses that still don't work, only get them deeper into

trouble

The trouble you saunter past, with your eye on the purpose of
your day, your heart on the task of your life with the allegiance
of your whole body and spirit, beauty and gifts, only you can
bring to a suffering world

I survived another night

the dilemma of letting go, the one i thought i mastered as a very
young child, the one that snuck back into this tent with my
name, to haunt me, as to, when my animated presence would no
longer be, still i simply trust my life to only recline in the
darkness, just rest, not run away, but come back

i have come back, the splash of cold water on my face, tells me
so, every part of me i find beneath the welcome shower, nothing
is lost, but what is gained?... it's too early to tell

only the day is early, along with the humidity, i cannot rush or
my impatience will only cause great waterfalls of sweat, wash
away all my cologne
i don't want to smell the way other's smell in their great hurry
their rush only leaves behind a wake of pleasure or disgust

already i feel lost in the commotion of whirlwind strangers
i have a sense i feel so together when i am sleeping, more
wishful thinking than actual reality

the day steals me from myself, yet, what is to be done
torn from nature i live disconnected midst confected insanity
each day i die a little more, each day i pretend i am something
other than what my bones, flesh, spirit, pulse tell me i really am

fear keeps me stuck on the mad speedway towards death

each night i gather what remains of myself, curl up with that

truth, the only real truth, the only real holy feel in my body

come morning find myself again kissed by smiling dawn

for a moment i feel real not dead

for a moment i am happy

In cold stillness, releasement

cold night, quiet
stillness seems… frozen
beneath white frigid sheets
calm currents yet throb winter's tender spirit

alive imagination with creative colors, waits
to be felt and felt
recognized
in the cold stillness an embrace of
like to like warms a body with freedom
one finds releasement from the weight of
law and order power contrived
a number identity to be codified for domination
concocted to perpetrate itself not life but
slow constricting death

a colonizing death injected from its rabid fingers
marks the doorways of our presence with its
ruthless brand of ownership

in cold stillness warm currents, affectionate
rise

wash us with its knowing, a knowing
that claims us as its own, shares a moreness
our bodies seldom feel, faintly remember

in the cold stillness we recall our worth
its warmth quickens a furry spirit
mixed into us in the womb
it dances through our bodies layered with lies
melts them to slip from us, dissolve into the snow
waiting to bury it forever in its eternal tomb

for a brief eternity we breathe a welcome releasement
from every collusion of deceit
transcribe words waiting for us to live
waiting for us to become our true identity
waiting for us to proclaim as poet guardian of all flesh and the earth
every meanness of demented creatures
gutted of any precious sense of real humanness

as bards of shared passion, preserve freedom from every
sly trick of apparent kindness meant to corral us all back
into bondage
obedient drones of disaster

but we must be vigilant, awake to the darkness
that slithers through night and day after
every person, creature, presence as food to feed
its unquenchable sickness

as poet guardians, the only required proof of our worth

-not some plastic license to grant acceptance-

we find our only true work, our only valid task:

keep alive the life fire to live more graciously together

when the cold stillness returns us to ourselves come the dawn

In the times of need

light seems bleak, only the shadow rises to answer the plea of

hearts stressed to breaking midst, the calamity of impending

death

No finger tipped lanterns blink a pulse of 'on the way', nothing

instinctive leaps to save the ones forsaken still to fend for

themselves alone

Who nowadays, lives along enough or even much enough in the

forest by the streams, along mountain trails where wonder

dances mornings awake

who feels the howl let alone release its prayer into the night or

day, conjure affection to catch and ride the wind back, kiss those

desperate for love

Who, who lives close to the truth flesh needs to breathe its

honesty, live actually not vicariously through books, feeling so

empty

words lacking wonder, can journey only so far before

their feet break, their legs collapse, since the ink in their spirit

has dried up, so they blow away as autumn or get swallowed by

Harmattan, without a trace or gift of welcome to the next
offspring of their dreams, now nothing more than skeletons
on the horizon, waiting to be anointed into the companionship of
those humanely living

74

"It's harder when you fight Your Own self", he said

Thou sayest it… the lies come easier... no one else is there to
question the ridiculous or the sublime, the truth or the 1/2 or the
not at all, the actuality of yesterday, or its webbed slick re-
writing to protect the innocent or guilty because the guilty
were or are still too close, too scary alive, maybe dead but still

their shadow lingers a nightmare that covers everything with the
film of their body, so thick you can smell it and not
blow it out your nose when it has gathered there
it will only leave when it decides it has done enough
enough you have had enough of, but don't have the energy to
snuff out

the electric bill has not been paid, after all these years you
always somehow came up short when it came to the 1-2 punch

but with age comes distance, with distance breath, with breath
some wisdom, usually the kind that can let things go
for the battle was never yours, it was a shame, or anger, or
feeling passed over, left out… the luggage of the other
the friend so called or parent absent, so called, but not yours
really, only yours when you picked it up
stuffed your pockets with it, trying to be good, trying to be

helpful, trying to be, to be, real in an unreal world, until
the day you realized it was not about real, but reading the scene
getting to know what was really going on, coming round going
down, yeah that one especially, so you would see and step aside
in time before the stuff coming at you plastered you

left you marked for a while, the while that felt like a lifetime
until the day the bill got paid, the light came on and shone so
bright everything real glowed honest, everything not burned
away, left no mark, no scent of history lingered, just space,

more space for you to take back, reclaim and know yourself for
the better, yes, for the better
regardless of how long it took to find ....

Jeff, are you awake? He Quired

Still up, yes, quaking, swallowing or trying to, without choking

on time, rolling wishes up into snowballs, magic can do that

despite the weather, despite the what or especially whatever

as flesh cannot stand a damned thing

Magic can outmaneuver anything or almost anything

can it turn ignorance into caring existence?

can it transform left to rot cities and their suffering folks into

spaces where respect, life, healthy life, flourish?

can it change the political urge from its totalitarian destructive

turn into the Armageddon of total profit in the stock exchange

for all existing life, every form of its myriad, majestic

incarnation?

can magic wrap of all forms of injustice, lock that away, let the

people free, leave death behind for a while, find life work

prosperous enough for decent housing, clothing, food, weekend

play, time to find one's human bones and flesh love embraced

share cherishment without worry or fear anymore?

can that magic happen or is all lost?

Is good a dream of yesterday, a fairy tale to tell our grand-

children about the once upon a time when things were good

not rot spoiled, guarded over by machines, stolen by minds rabid

sick with sole possession, offshore account of all the world's

money, total power, absolute control, almighty domination?

Could magic be strong enough to make it be the time when we
wrenched humanity from the brink of extinction by the will of
our own hearts, hearts full of enough of pain and sorrow, so full
enough to light anger beneath our ass and feet, move against the
greed despite the tanks, bombs, bullets, so at least many died
with a bursting hurrah of freedom, so more enough could finally
taste it for breakfast when light returned to bless once more
a new day for humanity, unfold it from brokenness, stand erect
in the grace of its right to belong, care for every kind of being
still alive to belong and flourish one and all on one land, under
one sky with well-being for each one, finally to be so for ever
and ever yes!!

July 4th! a 4th of What?

Life blood poured a poor sacrifice from poorer men

Spilled as one belief, one truth, one brother effort

Union of brothers, a brotherhood promise

Blood bath wash to spray away one oppressor

Only to be harnessed by a home grown one

Grand party for landed rich aristo-scums

Fancy dressed bullshitters of kites and wooden teeth as

low as they can come

So much for farmers uprising against lost land

An almost battle with the militia to get taxed for the whiskey brewed by

our hands

Oh, sure no rebellions to unsettle your Hudson River Estates

Large land tracts for us to work for your opulent tastes

July 4th! a 4th of What?

A bottle of booze to sooth the aches, bruised bodies

Condemned to a lower estate far away from your power base

Get wounded, get maimed, get dead from wars for more control with

Treaty Lies to Native Peoples, since Homesteaders would

be sent in to trespass, get maimed, get killed so the army

now could have reason to kill, slaughter, genocide

Carve more states from the limbs of the dead

Keep the South in splendid plantations, weekend cotillions, economic opulence while

Black people got labeled non-human, jammed into slave ships, to land on the sellers docket, get worked to death

Get raped, get objectified for medical experiments gynecological and every kind

Keep Northern mills supplied with cheap foreign and

domestic workers, even women and children could join in

Sure profit-makers for quick buck schemers

Hailed as holy entrepreneurs, Capitalist marauders

Historians crown in their mighty books as heroes of another kind of

Manifest Destiny

Users of every abuse, yet memorialized as heroes

We must memorize, think to emulate, become one day a neighbor with a house as large or larger than the ancestral acclaimed one next door

July 4th! a 4th of What?

Another excuse to try to white wash, forget the fucking mess we birthed, support, grant entitlement to use, abuse then throw away everyone, any living presence that's not got a "Blue blood Heritage"

Oh! Brothers and Sisters, if there's still a 4th left, there's no time to lose

Stand up, toss out what's cruelly obscene

Value each other no matter, color, class or any other superficial distinction

None of that matters when Life upon a scaffold stands itself ready to hang

 Since everything was left to rich politicians to do with as they pleased and wreck the place that is our HOME

When Love is the bounty, care the golden field because we along with all creatures have the whole earth as home not some state or nation or

some crackpot government

Life's the home for all to live through humble respect

Caritas, hospitable graciousness

Not Ego hubris, individual avarice

That's the ¼ left of this July 4th

Will our grandchildren experience it or curse us instead

For being fire-works fuck ups!

Drunken moo-cow followers without any human consciousness!

"Jump in!"

she yelled wave surfing, i was just about to when i got
swallowed by a shadow huge, a piece of history rose from the
sea, a piece of this country's buried stuff, thought barnacled
covered over too deep to drift up, too hidden for any kind of
resurrection, but conscience does not sleep, too many wounds,
ache and cry out 24 -7

gulped down, i found myself lashed to its main mast, whipped
by the storm, stirred by anger, grief, guilt by doing, guilt by
the association, guilt for sleep walking, guilt for not even
questioning, guilt for silence, guilt for ear plugging, until
the fire came this time, no longer patient "next time"
since, there may be no more next, since time is now, the past has
died already bereft

the future on street corner, sighs wanting the embrace of
aliveness, reverent affection, heartfelt respect, not just speeches
and apologies that are thought to clear the water, make amends
heal all the scrapes and wounds, bleeding, still bleeding since
not a day goes by, some hate monger, opens the same old
wound, and the blood pours, just pours, just sorrow and drowned
prayers, 'cause nothing is cleaned up, nothing gets cleared
nothing gets rectified, nothing gets forgiven, because nothing

really gets truth-ed, only dressed up in more lies, like politicians
in new black suits, wearing new smiles, smiling new lies, while
the ocean keeps the stories, holds the secrets and the dreams
and we can go surfing, but not now

i just blood let my conscience, i feel a wild splash, guess the
sharks got a scent and they are fast on the trail, no time for
surfing, better head for the beach, get the holy heck, out
here!!!

Keep the music sounding

we need melodic sooth, a new beat to reset our hearts
some electric feel, another kind so much kinder feeling to
remember to be human, real, not some shadow ugly, despite
mean fumed air

We are all the precious even if our bodies don't fit just right
need some coming to, to understand, know, respect so
anyone can go to the bathroom without fear, walk streets
proud to be, just be
share in the alive, poetry, art, music blood transfusion to clear
rusty histories out
the one picked by family, schoolyard, classroom, neighborhood
friends who don't speak one way, another behind your back

The sooth that makes the day work worth it, always have bucks
a few extra coins, do something gift-like for a close one, make
their gray turn a smile

Be a goodness beacon, so others can feel the light, shave off
those lizard scales that can tend to grow back overnight
attempt to steal the precious, so only the growl prowls
concrete sidewalk cemeteries, drives asphalt blood stained
streets, crying for remembrance, crying to end tyranny

The growl tries to drown out the music, soul food to incarnate
spirits, but the angel inside us, gives that look, it just curls up
blows away nothing, it really always was
false power with a gun, but inside a nothing empty
sorrow excuse for a lost life, big muscles, fat mouth just
lying its way through, instead of melting with the music
that brings all of us home, back home to the earth home

Our real only home, not what's put over her precious body
strutting so civilized
every step just kills what it tweets it loves, so love
becomes just a fast fuck, compassion an ass beatin', every night

So, the music, humble humans, sidewalk plays, a testament to
the holy, a witness to the truth, despite the pain, the horror
despite silence lip shut, turned head that sees only its problems
unaware of their suffering is the anguish of all despite
the this or that declension, vocabulary of place

We all answer to the music, the music that melts us back to the
axis, love center, beatitude blessed

We're all beat but still beautiful, just a hug will make us believe
follow the music together, forget everything we've been taught
let respect wash us clean of our stuff
have everyone become warm present music… LOVE!!

"Life is hard in this part of the world"

No rest for the weary
no relief for the already overburdened
the sun will continue to burn its will into you
the rains will fall harsh to remind you of your earth being-ness

The day will not laugh, the night will remain silent except for
the creatures who leave the imprints of your chores upon your
dreamless mind, so you find the more come dawn
the more you thought you already had completed, but forgot
the day already has placed its obligations at your door

Yesterday laughs when it spies your sad face
a breeze will slap your bottom into motion
get you over yourself, and out into the world, the world
calling you with its tears, its own wounds, its own dreams
to be cradled by you, kissed by you as you wrap it on your back
and bear it as its lover, the intimate it needs to feel complete
worthy to toll its hours, get sweaty, laugh and pray the time goes
fast
When time goes as fast as it only can
its feet are too small to run
its legs too thin to leap over the chasm of thirty minutes, you
would like to forget, but

that time calls you to embrace it, it needs your company
The we all around, even if they look preoccupied, stern with
worries, feel better catching a glimpse of you, and others you
know and don't know, suddenly find a second wind to
persevere, just keep going, without hope, just the pulse that
writes their name before their eyes, makes the journey of
whatever, about whatever, to wherever worth the while because

It was done and done as well as possible to make the day ready
for bed
feel good about itself and give you a blessing kiss goodnight

May the freckled wisdom

many of us bear not get lost when we sail upon

our brown curled leafy breathe

let it seep into the flesh and life of those left behind

an ecstatic reminder colorful, buoyant, flexible free about

what you and i, by the shaved age of time, discovered about

what is vital and what it is not to really be a human creature

So, the children and their children

(promise of our dented dreams, wishes twisted by mean histories)

while becoming the good they have in them and still to find

recreate through electric waves artistic our faint spirit through

their bodies

Put aside destructive ego whims, free imprisoned hearts, guide

spirit and mind to take up with filial dedication, eager excitement

creative tasks, to insure wellbeing remains within the moreness of

the un-imprisoned heart

in that way encourage and foster the only task, actual real and true

care of earth and others!

Memories

My pulse surges memories

my landscape no longer large

elastic quick, drifts slowly

to lick what puddles, remain where

colors dance to rhythms that

only pet me now the way

one of my childhood dogs would

flop its paw on my lap

look up at me with ocean eyes

not to go "out!", just to be seen

be touched to verify the poor dear

was actually alive and not dreaming

this creature was my spirit-guide in

disguise

Atop that low tide drift i float dismembered

into histories bleeding out their terror

they try to breathe but choke on all the murders

a penance, i guess, the way autumn returns to

strip nature of its pride, and us, despite our dis-

belief to have to bare all before a dying world

Even then our superior sense of self demands an audience

before silence we pout, act out, as if that would make

a difference, we forget nature is not our neighbor nor a
presence to be toyed with
i find myself as if at Savor's picking over stuff
my mind an after lunch poor excuse for
anything, let alone being aware, more
importantly, responsible for whatever
my fingers touch and how since so many
voices sound their pain or delight, or worse
annoyance, theirs not mine, they want an
answer from me, but they exhale too
sharp, others too gritty with that feel of some
possessive need, that steel cold breeze of
impatience to have what dark drama unfold
wanted, given, received, regardless of my
ability, even want or need to connect to the
script they stripped from their body

i hung them back on the wrack to sweat it out
by themselves, i was too apprehensive from
the burn with teeth to eat my flesh if i did not
move to a cooler, more humane isle of human traffic
presenting themselves in various appealing
frescoes of sensual attitudes

The sweaters in the women's section looked sharper
for me i need something warm, they seemed to
offer that, not the men's frayed elbows, worn
shiny chests and backs – not my kind of posh

It's autumn, i need to be practical
nature's clock is ticking away, moving earth
destiny, forgiveness
possibly a moment for lightening to gather
together so everything can finally fit without
tears, without hurting, without feeling dirty
without having any sense of having to pay-off
something
get your passport stamped after the uniformed
gunned-up attendant x-ray eyed you and
longer than you expected, wanted, as if
privilege once again abused its power for
some sadistic pleasure just because, it could

But i had my sweater, felt more cozy than
i'd ever felt before, i felt the kind of good that
lets you know you are, were and will be, worth it
no matter how those baleful autumn eyes appear
how sad that huff that swirls across your lap
forms a connective bridge, that always sought-after link
now present to erase all questions, annoying doubts
so, your name relaxed can now embrace you as never before
thank you for the honesty to keep-going, not capitulate to
the weather that threatened to wash you away, then with a
spray of firework colors say good-bye

Yes, those faithful nostrils always sniffed me out
kept me on track, stopped and redirected me with

a teeth-tight tug that wouldn't give up until i obeyed

the will better than mine

sat me down long enough to feel what i, you, we are supposed to

know before, we prance off into a winter coffin without

slight pulsed memories to cut the deep eternal, chill

Nature Mirrors Us

countryside frozen paints the heart

air frigid fierce meanness speaks

nature infected mirrors the most of us, despite

the few of us whose faith holds all flesh dear

whose pulse bears still the ancient flame of camaraderie where thrive

kind mouths, eyes love blessing

despite the cancer

sick minds anger packed, revenge vein riddled

whip into a killing frenzy like this frigid wind death screaming

no dream come dawn will warm to melt

only stiffen reality all the more coffin sealed

to hunt down the precious keepers of the promise

hate cannot stand what reminds it of what it's done

only slaughter quells the dread of evil

only blood inebriates conscience enough, but never destruction

that's the only heaven power, with its pitiful believers panting for

some crumbs of recognition, know

"No words, but sighs...why?"

sometimes it's the humidity, sometimes the rain, other times it is the
cold and snowy, blustery winds that cut softness

sometimes it is simply the weight of gravity, that tonnage that rests on
our shoulders, not the beauty of clouds, the sensual brush of slight warm
breezes

the heaviness of the murderous climate, where senseless death is being
perpetrated, killing acted out, bloodletting filling the plastic cups of
mad beings who cannot drink enough

the sacrilege against young girls and women world-wide
the death camps of Sudan, the red flowing streets here from the spent
life of precious beings

the slander of lies that pollute the air, darken minds, erase conscience
stuff mouths so silence thrives to allow crimes of all kinds to continue
so rich get richer, and the ones who vote lose more of their flesh to
the obese egos they allow to govern

maybe sometimes it is only the need for silence
the embrace of quiet to heal the body of all its wounds
gently rock the mind into peaceful sleep
the heart to lay down in fields of gorgeous flowers

smell the precious aroma of life

remember the precious

put another log in the hearth where perseverance cries for heat, so

it does not stiffen and crack into pieces of lost remembrance

sometimes it is just the want of those particular arms

to break the silence of affection

make real the existence of love

yes love, so words can once more blossom in the poet's breast

take shape on paper, become incarnate with that voice that frees them to

sail, lift up others to not forget the human work, and persevere...

Ocean

i try to ride the ocean, get no further than my thoughts
wind up in the same place as yesterday
i didn't like it then, i don't like it still, nothing changed it
overnight, and a new name via Prime won't do

Bad is bad, criminal is criminal, this green sea inviting
wavy smiles, erotic not shy, only cover but can't hide the blood
beneath the surface, the blood of tears, the blood of desire, the
blood a life sought to be lived in harmony, respect, wrecked on
some ego curb, cut up for somebody's plate of enjoyment served
up with hot fries, beach side brews

So, the fever rocks while the conscience drowns, sinks down, down
deep into the murky where no space for quiet, room peace or bed for rest
that elemental medicine to let flourish some gathering together

Tomorrow too soon will smash solitude, the surf will be rough
the surf will be ready, ready to scrub the dreams out of those
thoughts so, you go no further, or, the undertow will take you out… for sure

Our Eye

Creates circles

moist life feeding spheres

within them loving spirits birth our dreams

Those precious, delicate, so vulnerable, yet

strong elemental forms of heart truths

mind gusto, flesh desire, the something of miraculous

to keep us going with at least a ½ smile of

"it's worth it" on

Our awakening morning or what remains of our

tired, frayed, late night face still thankful for

another day, still precious despite, its snapped shoe laces

myriad swirls of aggravations, every piece of mail

you don't want, ever waiting for the one every inch of you

pines for, will still add, to the list of your night prayers

POWER: A POEM FOR GREGORY CORSO

The ground has power

The tree power

The air power

The mountains power

Water power

Above ground, underground, underneath

Unseen

Inside – out

Upside – down

Scrambled over easy oatmeal critters – power

Growing up

Walking around

Peeing

Crapping

Washing

Dressing

Tying shoes

Combing hair

Brushing teeth – not brushing teeth

Just sitting there writing a poem

Being late to work power

A cuddle

Kiss

Fondling, lovemaking, baby making or not making

Maybe just bed making

Sweeping

Berry picking

Taking down a mastodon is power

To cross the street

Share a lollipop

Stand up for the one called names

Left out, pushed around, beat up

Is power

To cool down anger

Let eyes see more than red

Hold back the punch

The curse

Put away the gun

Is power

To hear your name

Wake you back to life

Not traffic, exams, no job, crap job

Not the one that's really not my job

Is power

Power, power

Everybody wants power

Kills for it, die for it

Sells their children for it

What we take for power is

A manufactured product of mad mind

Chemtrail ego

Militated by knitting machines

Corrupted into currencies

Cut up into a wedge of apple pie

On barbed wire plates

Defended by knives, flying spoons

Atomic button bombs plucked from starched shirts

The shadow cast from fat-bellied creeps

Too up there, out there, beware

They own your underwear

Never flush their toilets

That's not power - That's atrocity

Power is a child on a bike who says 'Hi'

With eyes that stretch out to hug

As he just happens to pass by you

Another flower blooming from the same power ground

He's delighted to be in!

Promise turned ironic

sadly, stunts growth

lacking decency, it languishes in the gutter where chaos rules

meanness tramples goodness under its hoofed feet

i belt the memory of good around my waist

its sap-like strength glues me together

keeps me sane despite the anguish i behold

the slaughter that paints my dreams with horror

the 'rather' i want to do, i leash by my side

keep anger and grief in separate pelvic dungeons

if they can't smell each other, i feel less pain

i disregard the harpy's screams that rumor my dissolution

my humanity is not for sale, even if it means some clever

plan to make my death an accident, i will not be just an

appearance on this earth, but the most i could be as a human

free of my fear, the burden of not knowing where i belong

finally, aware that i was always home despite the ever unsettled

anguish of being an outsider to realize in death relationships

are the hearth of acceptance, the ever-moveable tent of

belonging!

Sad passion drips its tears

but cannot look down or back, it aches too much
to know where they went since
there's no way nor sense to return

Clouds steal the sun, how come pleasure must,
more often than not, be taken without asking
taken without even a smile, taken a purse, a cell phone
life at night, as if darkness has no eyes, no ears, it has
a memory, why do you think it broods heavy by
the fire escape, by morning leaves sidewalks and cars so damp

Just because no one can hear the night moan its grief, it's mouth
speaks louder than each night train coming to each station
bearing so many histories not just spray-painted bones to incarnate
inspiration, not just decorate the gates of cemeteries where bodies
unload, drift to their destinations, some cry because they heard
the news of passion taken, there's was too, too young, so many
apartments ago

That bruised and battered leather luggage bag, the one that
could not hold everything one wanted like, the child in me
the child i was, but only just the necessities, not the things
i loved, not the things i got slapped out of my hands, those 2 or 3
Holy trinkets i went to sleep with to feel some… affection

Self-Care Needs Time Too

it is no crime to sometimes shut the door

keep some beach space just for you

let the phone ring

tomorrow is another day, and another supposed

'end of the world' incident will be handled soon

as soon as i have my strength

as soon as i have my wits and being together to see and feel

i am tired of being a marvelous dinner for others

when i reach the table of myself, nothing is there

no wonder i have lost weight, more importantly

feel empty inside because i can't find my soul

"She Knows"

She knows, of course she
knows
alive her senses register
everything
she will detect the slightest
scent
smudge of cheek, if not, faint
left overs
of painted lips

Showers
quick and fast don't wash
everything away
anyway
she knows when you usually wash
has memorized
the habits of your day
any
change in the usual
sound alarms neither you nor i can
hear

We're too busy at being angelic
memorizing a

new script of fresh deceit

Little do we know she smells and feels
the slight stiffness of theatrics
who can really put on and act the make up
when
the scene is about the heart in
the balance

So
don't lie, just try to be yourself
with freshly painted nails she will scratch away
your façade
she knows perfectly well how to play, so

Before you know it, the show is over
and you are on the dazed street walking
without
your left nut

Don't come crying to me, fool
just be glad it's not your
Head

unlocks the forest of stillness, the place all bodies rediscover their
wonder, not just slavery to utility,

The place where relaxed flesh opens to consciousness of its beauty
marvelous form, unashamed presence in the world of forms and bodies

The place where the mind settles down, no longer a pumped-up rush, hectic
sweat driven, always ahead of the present amount, a panzer division
racing to conquer some Stalingrad in the dead of winter, exhausted
with little if any energy supply

The place where neutrality sorts out the real and imagined, the proper
from improper action, the duplicity of everything to make us tyrants
rather than more loving beings

The place where a tranquil sense of heart beat enjoys the slow breath
moving in harmony, not forced or demanded, with the ALL around

The place we find ourselves and cry with joy that we are no longer lost
a mere shadow of a thought about what we are supposed to be, but bathe
in the goodness of who we are, were once, and always meant to be
finally, can be, if we could only believe in the truth of silence,
the friendship of silence, realize our ruthless activities are only killing
our veins and hearts, our spirit, shrinking our very soul into the prison of
insane duty to an alien will, divorced from nature, a will that hates the

natural because it is just there, and just there in its majestic nakedness

needs to be exploited, made something to sell, make a profit, but not

for many only a gluttonous few, who, so addicted to more, can never

stop killing

The place silence reminds us we are not murderers, we are participants

with creation, participants to help our earth home flourish, not be

pillaged, raped with such ruthlessness, as if it's worth was nothing

because it had nothing to do with money except as nature-scene-art for

us to pay for, gloat over, remark how wonderful it is, so life-like

as we walk around with oxygen masks, or at least those who can afford

them, while those who can't, dissolve into the ground nameless

un-memorialized in history books as great discoverer's, inventor's

exploiters, political egotists who made their country great while

exploiting slavery in new updated ways

The place of silence unlocks our conscience to get off ourselves,
embrace
our place in the erotic intimacy of living presences all around us
that mystical gifting to allow all life to flourish as its form was intended
for ages or for simply a moment

The place of silence not just a specialty for the cloistered but for all of us

to find our earthly heritage, celebrate our enfleshed existence, safeguard

it and every other form that has its own fleshy presence
Silence the virtue that allows us to move with heart together with
the choir of other heart pulses in unison with our own, so we blend
together to make one grand symphony of JOY!

Simplicity of the real

one am winds rise and fall, unsettled tides moan uncertain
caught between whether to come or go

a conscience concerned about something unspeakable
discovers itself torn between good and evil, humans too nervous
to decide, try to deceive decision but decision is not an autumn
leaf cannot get blown away only settles a burr deeper into the
flesh whose ache only burdens more this weary body with the
burn of death, the specter at the before and after a life

reality weaves through its muscles good and evil words to speak
leave others locked up in hidden prisons of shame or honor
outcast or acceptance, rejection or affection, ignorance or
wisdom … purity is but a wish that cannot be a reality, our
frailty cannot uphold what's been bequeathed to us

to play, we costume up at knowing, act what speeches we can
find to appear as if we know when lightening sharpens its sword
between every pause, a desire peeps through an opening in the
clouds as if it could be born midst the thunder of a turbulent
heart already betrayed by a history of decisions branded into our
bones, etched on our tongues, so we say THEM, not the words
we want to speak forged by the honest heart close to the origin,
not yet afraid, not yet compelled to silence something vitally
attuned to another story gasping for freedom to be the answer to

the riddle no one wants to hear

no one would believe, since it's simple, does not require intrigue

murder mystery, stealth bombers, a life on a plot chained to debt

or segregates, imprison-gates, or concentrates like orange juice

or denies access since you're needed where you came from to

work cheap, for the us with capital letters

everyone's underwear is in a bundle, integrity gets stymied by

compromised backbones of will caught between hurricane

forces of competing desires, or secret night agreements, day

payoffs known only when you turn the corner, find your favorite

hang-out shuttered, discover yourself alone, faced once more to

choose death or sip from the cup of ½ a life, the deal that sounds

good, but always takes more than it gives

the gods always have their way, not the gods of sky or mountain

caves, tabernacles or fiery speeches, the ones that look like you

but can afford better cologne, who sound most sincere about

your welfare yet whose lips slice words to fit their own security

to navigate shifting oceans, serf winds with the ease of demons

the kind that rumble in us, devour our worth from the inside out

chain us to shame or revenge, so the penance of the in between

place remains incomplete, we remain stuffed in the darkness of

obedient oblivion, the price for our living, the feel to keep us

feeling better than some other entities, but never able to love become the moreness our original precious holds for us, follow that primal pulse to reconcile opposites, embrace both, finally BE the Simplicity of the REAL!

Soft lit day

gentle press against me, wished through the pages of my life
inscribed in kisses, laughter carved across our bellies

those few splendid chapters, what a wonderful liturgy of the
love we whispered for in all our night prayers, day wished sighs
during recess and lunchtime

almost enough, as if we could prove our worth and the lie that
love was not meant to last for either of us, false…
but see itself more than it is, more than flesh and bone can ever
be, before the largesse

we are not authors, only listeners at best
what is experienced is not to be taken as a war between good and evil
a wrestling match between failure and success, nor a gun barrel twirl
of philosophical roulette

we are precious beings on a winding journey of becoming, and at
any age or day, we find ourselves a bit closer to that fullness than
the day before, since each day we find and embrace another precious
fragment of our cherished self, we had to barter away or put aside
as children to simply get on

now more sturdy from all our badges of survival, we know a little better

how and who to trust and more vital to the cause of life listen to what
echoes as the more human choice within, no matter the sacrifice
no power position, wealth nor prestigious honor will count for much
on that last bed, in those last fleeting moments than to realize that
despite the cards dealt for us to play, we lived as real and true
as possible and bequeath that for those who follow

Stomach Beach Waved Stuck

a gravity, gravity, gravity stuck beach,

pressed, pressed so pressed hard electric fingers don't laugh, just poke

poke, poke oh, poke, so knife-like poke into this poverty flesh

without a voice but

for a pen, pen, pen so honest pen, to spill out what tongue cannot

not, not, type on lips, mouth to broadcast out, out, out beyond the

deaf, to feed the starved, emaciated bone bags cornered, street corner

cornered, shoe less but for the socks that arrived on their birthday

a smile toothless but no less happy for less weight is better

cross the street faster, faster lightning faster since socks hold souls

much better than buttered bread, and all the prayers on Sunday offered

some coin from the collection thrown our way, feed for birds who fly

fly, fly, bomb, bomb, bomb

but i don't bomb, just stare from day to day, through tenement

window eyes, watch the same pass by, by, oh, by, oh that fevered poke

almost made me sick, but nothing's in my stomach's left that gaseous

party place, burping after heaven's ads, so soft divine

empty now that place dusty now, now, now, nothing can last there long

since i've breathed the truth, can't eat the food, can't tell the lies pumped

down there from all those hot dogs, green beans and peanut butter sand –

witches, sweeping, sweeping, broomstick sweeping tears from clouds

clouds from minds, the only movement with that cheerful laughter

laughter, laughter, to break the gravity, gravity, gravity, plunging its

nails, banging its hammers, bodies down into beach, where bodies

pressed, pressed, oh so pressed into such coffin neat black suits

beach stuck without music only the screams of children dying from

from profit gutted bellies by pirates, pirates, pirates from all the holy
nations pure, pure, pure, so white pure holy nations, extending
culture, civilized bliss but the hand that does the actual work, work
work holds nothing, only middle fingered surprise, surprise, surprise
despite all their speeches, despite all their gold, spoke only the lie of
stomach linings drying, drying, drying, from all the constant rays
pushing shoving whatever's left, across the desola---tion, -tion, -tion
final kingdom of...depravity

The artist of any kind

exists one foot in reality light creates from nothing

her shadow a river flows over consciousness of pain hardened

outlooks dimmed by too many lost skirmishes with shame

He offers solace to beat travelers back packed with first grade

books of lies, homework done, yet in the margins lie scribbled

dreams of freedom that throb to breathe the wonder of delight so

close, yet for heinous reasons remain so far away

With her other foot in the darkness, She stays balanced by

shadowland knowledge, can see what is actually taking place

hear the actual meaning smiling words convey, since serpent

tongues sound so good, offer such affection for those discarded

to the curb unable to shine the presents they have to give

The artist appears to most a bizarre outsider, yet in truth she and

he exists between two worlds, tent in the space that holds the

opposites together, so the world does not rip apart from the

strife of outside, turmoil, the agony of internal doubt

Only the artist's creative pulse unlocks purpose for us to return

to rounds of mindless chores since no immediate benefit follows

only repetition of more until the siren sounds, the sun clocks out

The beat up, beat down, shift into reverse, the artist intact

advances to cool aggravation, redirect attention from the silence
of a world unable to answer our questions nor relieve us of the
scourge of our poverty or our wealth, She reminds us

We are bound to a more cherished truth: another day's honest
dedication to the tasks to which we find ourselves bound, and
return home with a smile aware that, despite every temptation
otherwise, we chose instead to take up our only real task: to
be compassionate beings, and not forget our fidelity to the
wellbeing of each other and our world

The Colors

Original from creation's finger forms us gorgeous, backbone splendid
each body wondrous gift receptive, whole, to nestle into this
vibrant tingling world before, the culture sculptor arrives to re-make, re-
form according to its own design, as if Life itself was not good enough
perfect enough to fit the picture of its ego

Our precious has been edited, redacted, ford motor line re-assembled
can no longer nestle, the flat cultured landscape becomes hard to
celebrate our original relational bliss, since now worth must be achieved
be accepted by another color scheme shrunk down to black or white, the
only ones digital computers can recognize, count, locate, track, then
shuttle us to our appropriate ordered place, pass tests of inclusion, wind
up with an outfit of a kind, but not a suit rewarded with degrees of
excellence, so freshly outfitted, living becomes a chore no longer a
loving liturgy, a dance in sync with the cosmic song

Speech cannot help us, our flesh contrived into jagged forms of statist
art, no longer conforms to Eden's dream, jumbled we attempt to unfold,
but only crash and wound into each other, attempt to apologize with
champagne dinners or another round of beers
if lucky maybe find understanding in another whose eyes untouched see
deeper than our own, whose heart less twisted industrial, feels more than
my pulse growing aware of its poverty

It pales before the splendor of trees and flowers, bird song and dawn, yet
still an ancient birthright strives within me, will not give up, despite the
daily struggle to be true and less a lie if not exactly forthright, persevere
despite the pain within that fights against the good, seems to undermine
my thoughts, my desire to let the colors beautiful, shine their affection

My feet sold out trip me, to murder me at the foot of my bed
leave me there bleeding, i hear an obnoxious laughter, i almost get
angry… but choose to laugh, laugh the last moments away
find happiness in that last revolt against the blandness, before
the dust closes my windows, rents the place i once called my home
leaves me curbside in a yellow bag for Tuesday's morning pick up

The empty behind made up eyes

Shattered, shattered, so much more shattered, everywhere rock shattered, bleeding shattered, tear less shattered since, the well of feeling has run dry, a litany of moans replace lanterns of glee once laughing, dancing, smiling the 'pretty' of feeling so alive so blissful once, no words could begin to explain the daily invasion, determined to spread the misery of vanquished hearts left cold in gutter shacks, abandoned to survive on their own

Desire's vital juice bombarded, only the debris of rape, stained glass shards of trust, leftover ruins of pillage, those nightmares pictures of rage insane, retribution against horrendous histories of neglect, merciless slaps, vengeful beatings pass on the life one only knows and will ensure others feel, so the whole world knows and feels what it means to live

Streaked welts, visible exclamation points keep the story alive their pretty broken flesh red bruised, toss black and blue framed photos of loveless days and nights, beneath the image and the smile

Lips remember enough of happiness to paint with kisses a believable passport of sincerity so, the intrigued accept the ad but not the person, shivering beneath paper thin scenes of 'happy', the attractive vibe that does not mean to seduce, just

find something of being seen, something of recognized even if it
is just worn words of an aged flirtatious script

A ping -pong playful tingling, a momentary high for something
never meant to be yours, just the pump up feel of the champ of
something before walking home alone only darkness hanging on
your arm, as speechless as stars, as quiet as your heart in the
gorgeous, sensual cemetery of your body

The golden kite flies

Allows harsh arrows to pass without harming
those relationships without which we would shrink from lack
of soft touch, collapse into an unruly dust ball marking everyone
And thing with our spleen before falling to the sidewalk to be
smashed into a cement eternity of constant kick of some foot-
gear piss, crap, spit and unfortunate blood mixed with gun-
powder, unclaimed wishes, a life short sheeted

The golden kite opens its expansive flesh to catch breezes
closes to surf the surface of undecided currents to avoid
as many wounds as possible, though kites like us cannot escape
this life with suffering some kind of woundedness, if not
undergoing the worst, getting trashed

Tortures fill the day, despite all the kisses that come to stop the
bleeding, street corner clogged with torments, especially at red
lights, when impatience boils over into murder with a knife
prepared to carve out so many ways to die

Such events wait to make history, big or small when they
decide to ambush the dreamy one, the pretty one, the
bound and determined one, so, by the time they reach their
destination they feel already more empty than full, less human
and they have yet to punch in, ready to punch each other
a habit for most, to feel the in-humanness would be an

interminable penance

Lunch offers little reprieve from the litany of insane mysteries
whose fingers smack painful irreverence to person, fill looks that
strip naked the one who stands suddenly a target for disgrace
grammar school still exists, only the desks and people are bigger

The golden kite flies a sign of redemption, a renewal that
requires no holding just the openness to risk feeling the
sensation of that roller-coaster downward surge "Oh Yeah"

That other-worldly feel doctors can't poke in to, or cut up or out
scientists can't measure, philosophers just repeat themselves
making up new vocabulary to mess with their phd students
theologians just sprinkle more water to bless wars, death
destruction for the kingdom, honor and glory of their god… for
ever and ever and ever… indeed read between the lines of your
history books, you will discover nothing has changed only the
clothes, only the weapons, only the slick language to fool us
keep us serfs fighting each other over this thing called racism
and white superiority so the only real business continues without
a hiccup to make rich people more rich

The golden kite that reignites "Oh Yeah" is not a lie but a
window to the truth to see beyond the fake theatrical, open up to
the energy that lifts legs, moves feet, to take those steps to keep

going, to rekindle the moreness nested in the shelter of one's pelvis, a moreness, a soul gift, one might say, without sounding too evangelical, meaning only to tap into that primal surge, earthy, moist, bird song, night howl to answer the kite

Enough gold lies within us untapped, just waiting for us to find a treasure that costs nothing but kindness, care, a shared banquet of affection so someone feels recognized, finds their 'human' again, realizes they still count, have worth without having to pay a toll, or taxes

And you know, with less doubt, perseverance thrives in you, you can let go of the false, embrace the true, become the earth waiting to play with you, dance and pray with you, embrace you within the grand round, the gift will not abandon you, but remain with you to heal and guide you to dwell within its abundance not the lie of prestige and status

The golden kite remains to guide us until the day the sky calls our name to take us to our place among the clouds, become teachers of wisdom not bookkeeping and deceit, there rest finally, in the real lap of happy

The late …

one on the bike in the window
crying blood tears cause you
are more than the late for dinner

the place guests remember something
ponder deep the rivers that flow through them
with their chill, their envy, their currents
naked kisses still, warm

someone notices their plates are covered
with something vaguely familiar
memories from the empty chair
from the window breathing freedom
finally
without traffic or lonely room crayons… that
only color
gone

The pain

So many names of it always follow me, i want to escape the
smell of their wet traces, but can't, they must smell my
adrenaline
their mouth crashes down on me with a fury of curses

The vengeance of time and hands, innocence and arrogance
strips me to my bones sore with truth, they abduct me

On the sandy bottom of their world i roll, scrap anyway every
lie, told, learned, memorized to pass the culture test, discover in
their moldy chambers everything i buried, to lessen the pain

i could numb it drinking cocktails of freedom, or so i thought, or
so i wished, but with dawn they woke with me, dressed me in
their burning

So much debris liters my conscience, no wonder my knees ache
i bear the pain from so much forgetfulness, my heart has
forgotten how to cry, or did i toss away the key to that door, in
the rush to get away, find in motion the way to feel alive, let
brief escapades do their momentary magic, since no place could
really embrace me with their lips, every tight luscious cord of
every naked promise pressed against my so innocent flesh,
nothing but guilt spilled from my veins when, the pain from the

skies broke my skin teasingly exposed, but not my will, iron fist
hard, at least on the outside

i realized i had to save myself, no one else could do that job, that
job that came with my birth, made, more difficult from the pain
of all the histories stuffed in my name, screaming at night to
steal my sleep, rage my day to slap my thoughts around, so i
spoke in riddles or pissed people off, finally too young to travel
decided to be as monastic as possible

That worked for a while, but the waves always found me, the
pain always threw me into their torture cell, at least i made
someone happy

i needed to chart the map back to myself, navigate through the
muck and mire of all those wet dreams, trace every lead back to
the tombstone that marked its redemption, left its ashen flowers
a salvation gift for me, when i finally bled enough to prove my
endurance, filled the cup of sacrifice with the last drops from the
wound
no longer running, or begging, or pretending just there
as mysterious as the night i was born
as bold as the day that sought to accept me
that day i was stolen from its hands
that day i got mutilated
that day i got abducted from myself

The penance

a swirl of images grip me for a journey

it turns out to be quite a ride, past and future collide in

the place night, mares sweaty, run out their spleen

drench me with their blood, menstrual hot from birthing some

other part of me, a part i did not realize, never knew, was hidden

from my inner eyes, obstructed by all the ads and crap that

cluttered up my outward seeking ones, the ones that provided no

map, only sights, selling tickets to different ways to play the

game of ahead, get more stay alive, better, if only i could stretch

my luck, but its salt-water-taffy-ness is old, my limbs only move

with the wind, my body with the ocean sound

a leaf of autumn glory fell, its colors spoke to tell me about the

time i lived in the belly where shadow sounds danced, and dusk

night light scanned damp landscapes, the place others had been

left notes, i could not read, only feel stone places that marked

where they once slept, before somehow not making it, wanting

it, but not making it to taste and feel

so invisible hands through the waters splashed to grab me, rock

me into the labyrinth of disgruntled seasons, sad days of deep

mourning anointed me with, the penance of unworthy, to work

through all my life

The truth

Parking lot cars, church benches, beautiful woman incarnate
open a foyer door…

Am i dreaming? Or does this sketch attempt to tell, The Truth?
the truth so hard to type on lips, blow out with breath to smack
your face silly with its Reality-Wet-STING!

A too late alarm since yesterday needed the backup, real
vocabulary to fight off the assault, but NO! As Always! had to
to do its best with sparse ammunition, no adequate reserve, not
even some baskets of rotten fruit to distract righteous feigners,
polished programed liars to stop, catch their breath just long
enough for one to lock a door, regroup, but this was not the
occasion for such mercy, as it turned out…

Such is Life

You can't find your car, the church bench breaks from the
slender weight of your ass, only a skeleton appears
laced only in spider webbing, no door opens

There is no door for you, after your 69 years of suffering
ignorance, it's time to step over, into The Truth-----

Just keep your mouth shut!
Watch your step, Damn it!
we don't want anymore, hurt, before your Time, you're
disappointed, wrecked, enough
already!!

The Way Waves Splash

Years melt with the rain
Memories spread across mind
Landscaped finger-painted colors

The way waves splash
The last word strolls from
The high bell tolling

Your lips change sharp with the day
Stitched by sunlight
Scratched by the tongue
Into a bag
Full of games and toys
Vegetables and bad boys
Undressed girls bend from
The hurricane swirling wind

The way waves splash
The last word strolls from
The high bell tolling

Those eyes that kissed me
Back to life
Sucked me out from

A desert
Into the doggie day
So furry raw
Purry rough
Unforgiving by
The slam of doors
Shots of bullet teeth
Nipping holes in the
Laced up closet
Where the unbuttoned heart
Wanted to discover
Forbidden delight tucked
Away where shadows play

The way waves splash
The last word strolls from
The high bell tolling

Between skipped beats
Your heart falls into the
Shivering palm of my
Short breath
Scared of the night who's
Fingers growl to strangle me
Rob me of winged fire
Cloud side busted tear
Rusted curbside sigh
Laughter joking with itself for

Crying over everything it wanted

The way waves splash
The last word strolls from
The high bell tolling

The word i cannot escape

floating remains the only remembrance of my childhood
the word i cannot escape
that buoyancy, despite sharp waves never-ending, even when
that sea caught me at birth with is watery hands
try to calm its rage, relax its urge to power
momentarily remove its bully gloves

still, only the buoyancy of floating has kept me alive
as if my body bound to live would not surrender it-
self to that sea

despite ugliness and grief, the nervous silence of absence
that creates distance, makes one a stranger beyond
the realm of belonging, so one watches, picks up cues
about how to fit in, get along, without making a sound

happiness did bend to kiss me, leave its mark of affection
over my chest to refresh me, sturdy me, focus me on
the larger fresco beyond the burden of life
not forgo the search for the solace of worth
its deep concern came at times most needed a welcome guest
to know closeness not just the ambivalent touch of shared
quarters due to inclement weather
to lighten the monotony of days packed with senseless tasks

with little merit than the sweat of labor that never reached
their promise, never fulfilled, only repetition of the same
activities, the only difference, different names
fulfillment seemed a promise as distant as the sun, the moon
the stars, a comet rewriting fate with the sigh of a heart

still my heart did not stop, my body quit, they knew better than
my mind, our worth lies in that fervor for life, that forward surge
that does not surrender the power of perseverance to any person,
unjust law, the oppression of domination, the shame of a class
system that places one on a higher or lower rung of a gilded
ladder with ever new rungs that bite fingers, stab palms into a
soundless scream though it bled from my mouth

it became clear early on, if it was heard, no one would hear it, if
they did, do nothing about it so, the laborious climb became a
never-ending sacrifice of so much preciousness with little if any
reward if reward would ever make one an authentic human
being

they exist, but one must be in the right place to experience
the recognition that resolves desperation, heals the birth cry
never answered, let o being really know the pulse that trembles
through them is real, not an aggravation no medicine can erase

that warm quaking is the cosmic fire that keeps us alive
buoyant, ever faithful to that integrity, persevere to the end of
one's breath

realize their best was always being as possible as ever, real as
one could ever be despite, the unfortunate fate of finding
themselves tossed into a ruthless sea

know at the last, those who do not bargain their humanness but
persevere to uphold the cause of all flesh not just their own
the aroma of roses will anoint them, not merely the stark
darkness of burnt ashes

There be a smile in the stillness

sweetness in the fold

a clam bearing up to a sky now open

no barrier of separation

no roof to shut one out

There be a smile in the stillness

reprieve in curled up arms

stiff brown, darkened prickly, but

aren't we all when we get old even though

we can laugh, laugh more than frown

since, what the hell, now we know for certain

laugh or frown ain't gonna change the outcome

one day coming for us all

So, there is no need for worry

there is no need for tears

there is no need for struggle

no need for a battle any longer to hold on

cause, there be a smile in the stillness

a sweetness in the fold

just listen to the autumn leaf

listen to the edges of its song

relax n' hold that leaf to your heart

may take a while, 'cause you may need some
time, to slow down n' settle down to the
easy stroll of the sun, the relax of soft, sleepy air
freedom of unburdened mind, no unpaid bills
pressing a hot iron on its weary back
only the softness of a curled leaf kiss
that long-awaited feel removing every burden
leaving room for that smile in the stillness
that sweetness in the fold

These days a sequence of silence

despite my touch, my kisses, my whispered questions, despite that
churning purr that identified my heart as THE heart climbing your
stilled mountains to reach your eyes before they closed and locked
from the inside out, obedient to the will of that willful cosmic force

Ever clever and so able to cramp its dominion over your landscapes
its crimson seal with midnight troops of clenched fists to insure
every inch of praying flesh, squirming dream, rebellion barking thought
would feel and feeling know, and knowing remember its rule would

Come and last until the last of its work was not just begun but finished
with another set of red earthen epiphanies, whose mystery glyphs, con-
ceived from moon time doings would be added to the collected works
ever being collected deep within sacred caverns where painted stomachs
rest vaulted till, only the trusted voice of damp journey speaks, unlocks
your mouth, liberates every captive to run off to find their matching
brand of freedom

You slip into that slight seam of surgically sliced flesh, the way you
unzip yourself from every layer of every year of your body where lay
every corpse of your history

Secrets always find a tongue, whether i give it to you or you crotchet one
for yourself, since we cannot find redemption without some other

intervention to crack the icy silence dripping from our hair, our mouths, fingertips, our naked belly buttons

That infamous monument that marks the spot you were told i 'once Saved you', and you 'once saved me', but neither of us committed such a sin against the other

Something more than us, something cosmic acted upon our presence and Shadow, to test the mettle of our Life Fire, reverently chart a middle way through darkness and light, matter and spirit, sound and silence of a never-ending test, never a quest brave, misbegotten minds bequeathed us

Silence did not rob you, i could not answer when you whispered: "So much i wanted to say but i've fallen into the silence you once saved me." … There was no option, we both had frightening silence to melt when we were strong enough to hear its truth, and live to save, each other

This gray day (Revised)

turns a windy eye

so we know her warm mood is not here to stay

a slight gift only

for having taken her stormy punishment without

wiggling or too many tears,

but to remember it is the season for mending

the time to make amends

learn a bit more about one's ways that sour or delight

water life or leave it behind to strangle from thirst

in the desert land our shadow casts, yes, absence is not only cold

but can be scalding hot

fierce with its sword of vengeance, scour of wounded pride

chilled fingers lead to the place i must wait for your arrival

practice patience

as frosty winds, grown sharp from the thrust of their energy

sting my face and hands, penetrate my coat and slacks

reach the holy places play with them laughing as they huddle afraid,

or dangle bold

dare the frost to stay aware the frost won't last, can't last

the belly, backside thigh lands are too warm, and will in

time rock the frost into eternity while

i with the we of all my colorful kin continue to breathe

beneath the elements that make the roof of our home, provide our food enjoyment, frolic love making wild as we roll together remembering summer with its naked pleasures since this gray day will not sit still relax or sleep but continue to turn its eye so windy ooo...

142

This photo catches you and

all the different histories that roam the landscapes of your deep

heartlands

they peep from your forest eyes, i can see them, i smile, i am not afraid

of the faces they make, the tongues they stick out

all they need is understanding, no more terror, just gentle holding in a

world that has lost its way and forgotten kindness

i see their teeth, hear their menacing growl, but i sense they will

not bite me, they will instead wait for you to write a poem to act out

the frenzied pain of their own braided anguish that won't give up barking

no matter what you do to make them stop

often pain feeds on pain, as much as it kicks love away, it wants love

to stand there and stay with them, suffer the testing my eyes see through

there are histories that plague us, because they cannot but help to make

everything around them suffer, as if that would compensate for the grand

damage to pride or some other glorified sense of self, that original fault

they had nothing to do with, but because of fate found bequeathed to

them, the same way even now i suffer the penance for some sin i did not

commit, does not belong to me, but was caught on my doorstep trying to

catch its breath, when it should have kept running to catch up with the

velocity of the wind, escape justice or its shadow brother, prejudice, or

worse it's other brother, power

such ones, most likely the cause for me to take the beating across

my flesh stripped bare so nothing would interfere with the pleasure the

one delivering the sentence wants so fully too feel, feel it to

engorgement, feel it to cosmic explosion, scream that primal roar

crumble every pillar supporting what's left of goodness, while forest

fires, sadistic wet, swallow what remains of beauty, level everything,

lock everything under the prison of a singular will, yet, other histories

remain that remember the truth, protect every bit of testimony to one day

reveal the truly guilty, liberate the truly innocent

Those lavender times

Paint rich heart colors that intoxicate us, make us forget that
nothing is solely what it seems, no matter how much it wants to
be100% true wool, that doesn't exist anymore, nor for the one
who whispers it into your hungry ear, starving for any sound of
love, affectionate touch, no matter how high tide crashing rough
come morning red or purple marks may still broadcast what you
were up to under the stars, so

Despite the hot weather, you discreetly cover up to hide what the
scoundrel left all over you as if to claim you, but your girlfriends
know, his pals cheer and slap his back, the both of you costume
up to look as mature as possible, yet time is younger than the
both of you, if added up together wouldn't pay for dinner, let
alone the bar tab of just beer nuts and chips

Lavender is grand, sweetens everything with its magic, playful
words hide their double meanings; they speak a truth but miss
the 'nothing but', since neither of you are seasoned, ever washed
each other's underwear to get a whiff of lies waiting in armpits
under the tongue, beneath the eyelids, those invisible creatures
marred by histories, some brutal, some slightly more kind, yet
each one leaving behind some bundle of rats eager to chew up
some good in you, replace it with some crap that can spin in you
if you are not careful, muck things up for you, like friendships or

jobs
Now, some other parts of your not so glamorous history not too
difficult to touch you might share by a kind of grown up version
of "i'll show you mine, if you show me yours?"

Some can be massaged to sleep when kisses light starry candles
fingers massage the night to grow, become moist with promise
answer the fevered heart plea, unleash the cries and howl, that
ecstatic holy chorus of satisfaction, so you collapse mere ashes
of lavender yesterday
wake up to the "NOW" once last night's future, now, the present
with breakfast and the bill

Sure, those promises young and hearty leave in the moment
spoken, honest claims, but with no insurance policy, only partial
truth, well intended, that one would share all the days that would
walk you 2 arm in arm into gray hammock-ed, graceful swung
filled memories

The word sure promised till the bill came due, made clear there
was more than 2 beneath the sheets, that shot heard round the
neighborhood, the unexpected shot, that bullet bleeding silence
as one flapped tormented in mean winds of tornado departure
the other covered only in tears, vacant from thought, empty from
heart arms, absent from view, but there was more than 2, now,
there's no longer 3
Only the incense of Good Friday lingers, bears the remains of
ripped dreams, so much for the completeness of the fit thought

just right to last for-ever

So much for lavender wishes of tangled tongues, the giving, the
forgiving, the dusting away hints that things may not be the
everything made up to be, the mind reviews of all those scenes
that cannot change the detonation that just thrust you into
Hiroshima time
You have your 1/2 of the tab but the one with the other is
evaporated milk, you a rainforest try to find yourself, hands
sweaty anxious, fingers bleed fear, heart anger pounds
mixed with shame for not reading things, trusting, hmmm
the harder slam to heal

The lavender time's gone, only you in the room left with the cat
the cleanup and worse, the penance of blue windows, the one
each generation passes on to the other to complete with some
hot pepper, mixed with guilt just to be sure the message gets felt

Tossed wish lost at sea

Bone of fractured bone, flame of battered heart both chained to the weight of my name, the only identity to give them some excuse to claim to be real, not lost in the currents that crack that wish in two, bleed away any connection with intimacy, simply float the fate of larger currents ruthless in their will to dominate forge an identity by unquestioned obedience

Midst the slash of circumcised waves, i bled a hostage to darkness, silent, but for the treachery of footsteps more silent than the humid breath closer, maybe imagined, still so real

Each tick of the clock counted away the length if not breath of my own presence that in time stole the tender blankets, the only cover then from the meanness of the place in which i discovered myself tossed into with no defense but for observations of every sense to note, for that time called much later, to better remember attempt to make sense of all those primal meanings of the silence of obedient doing that spoke nothing, left no meaning but the one i was supposed to know and not bother anyone by asking about it, just get along, forge a life out of nothing like the adults said, the "good book" claimed, from that make my own supposed success

But the silence was scary, silence had no arms to hold me

the world felt cruel always with its hitting and the crying from
neighborhood yards or left open windows, then school where the
innocent could be beat as well as the guilty, that made no sense
The covering that was supposed to protect didn't last, left me
naked before the world, an exposed toy to play with, a target
to cream with the shame and pain and anger and vengeance for
anyone's lost happiness, their grief over being cheated of the
goodness they thought they deserved but never really got

Oh, we had christmas alright, we all did, or most of us, but never
the one we really wanted, always the one our tears would rock
us off to sleep, the one we felt abandoned to the silent night that
was never that holy, only lonely from the chilled and wordless
feeling of being orphaned to a place that offered orders without
direction, routines but no sense, just rules to follow but without
Loving embrace, actual affection, only a hole grew each year
bigger, a hole that became the emptiness of my life, the close
but no prize to every endeavor, the table for one despite the
laughter of the crowd dancing in tight spaces, bumping into
each other through the music and partying, the look and
sound of happy, the pleasant snapshot of inebriated joy that
passed and still passes for genuine aliveness

When our parking lot eyes connected, i could tell i was not the
only one who felt something was missing, but everyone said every-
thing was... good

Walk every day

for some length, for some time, even if it is the time of a broken
shoelace, the whisper of a sneaker caught in the crack of a thought,
the one you have been cooking on for days, but
will not rise, only makes faces at you, to mess with you, not have you
write it yet, not yet, it just turns into a pointed stick, pokes your side till
it bleeds, then snarls at you, and you want to toss it out the window
but
something stops you, freezes you on the corner of lights, exploding
their truth, washing you in their secrets, you stand there for some length
catch your breath, regather your feelings, stuff them for some moment
carefully in your back pockets where they begin to cook breakfast

never realized you had a kitchen back there, yep usually it operated
Thursday mornings, see it happened now, things are getting better
all the little animals, cats and dogs, first graders and doctoral candidates
gather behind you, shoving each other out of the way, until you turn
around, and eye them with your soft-spoken spear-like voice, scream
through the curtained windowed street: "Stop acting like beasts!!

(you are not above them or below them, just stay in between, don't lose
your pants, keep it buckled, therein lies your salvation, your sanity, your
blessed humanity not your unleashed murderous, selfish madness,
enough of the killing, the earth chokes on the blood, sinks in the deep
waters of too many tears whose sadness pulls my very bones down to the

shipwreck of humankind, earth molestation, complete depravity thought

the only pain to avenge when the only medicine is your own arms

around another wounded one trembling

let the warmth pass from you into them, warm them back into their

common flesh, find their common home, and there realize they have

spent too much time circling in the desert oblivion of superior desire

 an overdose of ownership, the pride of better than, that blinds us to the

 the true worth of our presence, and the reality no one needs a doctorate

in relational living to love themselves and then to love others

see in them the promise of one's self, just needing a hand to pick them

up, dust them off, to find the path, rich with feet and stories, the sweat

of smiles, the sunlight of faces happy to walk with, beside you every

day, for a second of giving, a moment for appreciation of the body that

makes us real, with goodness we can incarnate not just for a walk

not just for some time, but for longer than some can hold a smile)

and, you, while walking down the sidewalk, find on the pages of clouds

the poem you have wanted, sought after, cried after, right there waiting

for you to walk only for some length, only for enough time for it to cook

and serve itself to you...

We are all Immigrants

We may have an address, but we have no home

The more we find out the truth, the further away we become
from who we thought we were
the further away from the worth
we thought we carried in our pockets
the value of our dreams
the wants of our expectations
the reality of the very morals we were told were foundations for
honest living

Not until private reason wrapped up in its self-concern dissolves
into the vast acceptance of empathy will we witness
capital ownership, power, greed burn up in a blaze of alleluias
then feel the earth pulse in our bones
the land welcome us equally as one of Her own

When we discover our worth in the eyes and flesh of the other
will we find ourselves at home
will we no longer be refugees hungry to belong because
finally, we will be settled in a place not to own or claim or
possess, just welcomed beings wherever we stand
residents embraced by the gracious goodness of the gifting
Earth

What will be left besides empty space?

you will wind up torn lace of memory

i crumbled dust of that yesterday that bore us

on its shoulders as proud to be as honestly alive

as ever we could be, so narcissistically enthralled

So happily, unaware of the blood stained deep in our clothes

the unspoken debris inherited from our ancestors that soiled

us more than our playing in the dirt

Dirt had nothing to do with their doings, it could only watch, or

close hard its eyes, plug up its ears, try to feel less those painful

tremors, anguished screams of life so horribly abused

landscapes raped of their beauty; lives murdered for the ego

want of more

the taking, not to fill stomachs with necessary food, but pockets

with more than they could carry just because

The foot that sailed over from another place, when stamped on

the land, what was another's was so no more so, 'cause

wherever the booted foot stomped, whatever was there, whether

another's or not, became the sole property of the boot, whatever

the boot wanted could and would be done…

   'cause whatever doing was ever wanted

    was ever good, by whatever means

conscience had no say, only obedience to the boot

the doing of the boot was all, the doing invented, tweaked
 "new" or "improved", the practice of doing almost never
honest, mostly done to scheme, finagle, steal, cheat…

all the better to shame, outwit or just see what might happen if it
were done… then scare others into giving without having done
to them what was done
   to another, or place, heritage, promise
   ancestral legacy long kept sacred, since
   place cared for people, people for place
    people already there respected not
   considered worthless, nothing or trash

Pull another thread anyone, smell the lives unworthy because
    not of the land-owner kind
     wealthy pompous kind
     business savvy kind
    professional arrogant kind that
built their lives, homes, fortunes on the backs, bodies, bones of
others by the unbearable treatment of those thought only born to
     serve, slave over
    meadow and field, homestead and hearth
    not indentured to work off their debt,
     no matter if free, if able, if artistic
    if keen minded, inventive, loving no matter
     well now make it matter

Pull another thread of your bloody clothes feel the lives willed
to be ever those beneath, called ignorant, lazy, too sexed, un-
wanted So,
no matter what freedom might come their way, it would
somehow always be taken away, So poverty would seem their
forever curse not naturally inherent, just socially enforced…
ever be their fault, the blame for the devil mischief played by
others on them, no matter what, they were only to be out of the way
with god's blessing intended to make the wealthy more rich
keep the middle and lower classes safely at bay

No matter what they do, or other allies might do… for their
                  good, their health, their prosperity would

slyly be taken by new fancy laws, as one was imprisoned on
"reservation" land, the other discovered that
        despite their sojourn north, the land may have changed but not
                          the landscape
both places were racists, just one plainly showed it, the other
                  rather righteously, tried to hide it

Keep pulling there's much more to pull to release you from what
bindings you know, the bindings you don't, the ones ingested
          So, each of us somewhat grows up never really to know
                  see, feel, hear what it means to be the other
when awareness awakens to arouse, make alert, begin the task
    to sledge hammer yourself out the rings of sly supremacist Saturn
Feel so proud, wonderful, human only to discover another one

thicker than the other, more bold than the other, more socially

politically, corporately entangled than the other, your hammer

breaks, your muscles weep for yourself

what about the other living in landscapes of bullet meanness

from outside and within, when hurt so deep, turns scour

attacks its own, hands over its own hates its own

and worse itself, sees no end to the living death of hatred

So, keep pulling…

those threads will pluck up ancestors related or not who still live

by force of voice, muscle of world armies, homeland police

those who every morning dress their conscience in gray

to insure the copyright of ruling owners on your body, mind

spirit, twitter thought, fb function, messenger feeling remains

THEN KNOW

the entire world feels the same stamp

lives the same charm, behaves the same

religion of thinking, regardless of the label

How voluntarily do we give over the earth, the way we give

over ourselves and others close or far, until possibly

We

discover the truth, get the full dose of murder,

assorted ways to kill

feel the multiple realities of death, landscapes of destruction

garbage water, crap air, unconscious able creature killing

with unforgivable hubris

committed unforgivable crimes

against every human being

know how the real culprits

absolved themselves, indoctrinated us, as if

they could charm us enough with perfume never to someday

wake up to finally smell the stink of our own poverty

with such hubris think we would always be clueless and foster their belief

secrecy would be the surgery to memory…

make everything "nice"

for them

When do we arrive at

ourselves, know no longer vaguely but with surety
this animated body with my name is solid, accept its reality as
valid, the presence that tents within its flesh, good

When do i arrive at the place to speak in first person no longer
use the third to hide behind its shield

When do i arrive at the place to accept my aliveness despite the
ever present scary mist weighted down with questions, despite
the fact i have survived to write quite a story regardless of
affection's lack that left its scar, tugs at me sometimes when it
needs from me the holding it never received when needed
reassurance to let go of the lies of nightmares that grip me in their
storms of vicious doubt about my very right to exist, to be
myself without some vague guilt i was someone else's penance

When do i arrive at the place to come to myself, enjoy the
fullness of my body, my existence in a world that ambushes that
surety when its defensive radars detect i feel safe, believe
enough love exists to continue to be the next step for my pulse
to maintain faith in my forward motion for the sake of the truth i
accept rather than believe the degradation of the
commodification creed of the culture i happened to be tossed
into, swallow, became

i am a rebel, was one as a child somehow aware things were not
exactly right, even before reading Camus, Dubois, Baldwin, yet
unable to take a stand then, too afraid of the pain wielded by
adults, overwhelmed by the kinds of the totalitarian authority i
witnessed and the brand of power expressed by their position
over the us who had yet to earn their proper place

Maybe that is why i never felt at home, despite the fact i was
born on wheels moving so often i could never stay too long in
one place, so motion could not ease my spirit, comfort my soul
that cried with an unquenchable yearning for something i could
not find in books, in various vocations, various locations

Motion only postponed the inevitable question that would arise
deflate my ambitions, cause that flat tire of defeat, pump it up
load the wagon once more, to the promise glowing over another
hill…

Still i ask myself now, close to the porch of elderhood, when do
i arrive at the place i come to myself, settle down in the gray
weary, find comfort in worn age, hope finally sitting in one
place, since my body has charged me to "SIT! Or ELSE!", will
provide the relax i need to answer the last questions, knit
together the loose ends that cause me grief i don't need, i am
in touch with enough pain of the world, now that my life has
slowed down
This poem itself is an attempt to come to the place to be that
Holy Liturgy, the place that allows the peaceful coming

together, since all the hot embers of old issues have cooled
some no longer make sense, some have left, deciding to stay in
another place

So, when do i, or anyone else, arrive at the place we come to
our-selves, only at the appointed time, the one each of us has in
our heart with its alarm ready to call us to the place of our
meeting without shoe banging, yelling incriminations, spitting
slurs, just peaceful space to rock, relax at the edge of serenity
able to sip the goodness of what was done, what could not be
done, what could have been under different circumstances
incense the guilty and the guilt

Simply relish the now as it is, forget what could be, the past is
gone, its testimony written as best as it could have under all the
weather conditions, the seismic quakes happening then

Now is the time to know better or possibly befriend for the first
time, the one you always wanted to know, forgive, embrace with
affection you always wanted to feel and feeling give, aware now
not just pound chest 'mea culpas' but do now what i, you, we
can to shift the love axis back to its proper place cut lose every
equator that bound and cut us off from each other, so our
children finally see another world to be their precious selves

Who is true and not just aimless

You can tell who is real and honest by their eyes, they are present, so awake you could brush your teeth in them, not like the usual traffic eyes, glazed donut or boozed up, 1/2 mast somewhere else eyes

The wanderer non-aimless has a purpose, you can see and feel it but you have to be with it to get it, not off somewhere else, if that's where you live, you're just going to drift an endless postcard with one address stamped over another but, no home to call yours, no body to claim as yours, cause you had one but lost it since, the truth there was bologna too thinly sliced, or dust from another's jacket, not worth the reading of anything inside too harsh or cold for even a coat, after so many beatings, you might wonder what you did wrong and how come nobody has told you, unless you are the designated but without a parade whipping post, so truth comes sideways, a smashed bottle of drunk wine
You have to grow up quicker than the seasons allow, but you don't live in seasons either, so you get sharper than a pencil start reading the air, eyes, faces, noses, bodies, there's a language to each one, it's not too hard to translate since feelings have a way of connecting, broadcasting real far so only sleepwalkers miss the real and walk right into an ambush, maybe not meant for them, but most days, anybody will do

So, you get with it, begin to read the weather behind eyes, what's
tensed up in the face and body, when the mouth contorts a
growl, the tongue a dagger, or a raging fire, out to scorch any-
thing or one in its path

Now, there's the truth worth learning, there's the truth getting an
A+ for, there's the knowledge that will get you through the days
and years, make sense to navigate the street-less world, manage
to be able to get some cash when things are too lean, feel an old
shed about to fall and crash a mighty hurt

The day by day knowledge sharpens senses so, you can smell a
tornado about to land or a pack of lies despite the smiling face
eyes sparkling like candles on a birthday cake
The knowledge seeps into you to let you travel deep behind the
layered sidewalk ad, textbook meanings, recognize they only
tell you what somebody else has confected as truth, possibly
jacked up to give themselves some advantage, it's called power
over you, lock you in their pain prison so they're no longer
alone, but have someone to play with, bully, burn, abuse so
they feel so much better and go out, have the fun you always
wanted to taste, but because you didn't listen up, wise up, you
wound up a fish fried wasted for too long of your life

Who will bury Memorial Day?

Spitballs and punches on the bus ride home

Book bags bulging homework as if bearing quadruplets

All those subjects and of course religion as if that

Would ever make me holy and less guilty, ashamed

A useless slob, but for god's merciful drip of

Redemptive grace, make me, once more feel so good

Till i caught some short-skirted girl bent over

Just tying her pure white and black saddle shoes

Lusting, lusting, happy lusting, oh damn!

Another late afternoon Saturday walk to church

For confession to clean my sin stained conscience

Gym class, boxing, wrestling mats, throw down, pin-winning point

All the balls one could play or not, slyly notice in the shower or not

Just quickly splash and dry, run off to class with straightened tie

Kennedy wanted us smart, healthy and spry

Little did we know, we would have our war

Almost like our father's, called Johnson's War

Our war, to prove our patriotic grit, masculine strength

Win at all cost, get a chest medal or

Coffin reward to carry one Home whole or

A sacrifice in splintered pieces

The medal that proved our courage and guts, platoon loyalty

Killing lust, to kill or be so, dodge the kill… to kill

Survive the killing rage and spree

Hopefully, this time for once and for all, bury Memorial Day

Return to quiet except for the dreams

Be an outsider in a foreign land, one that once echoed friend's jokes

Backyard swings, cook outs, Home, laughter, sentimental photos

Ice cream, beer, first this, first that, first wedding date

Now the only sense marching out of memory's haze

Arrives at the bar with what remains of Platoon Brothers knit solid

As night to day, death to life, night sweats to the insanity of office work

Yet, trained to patriotic 'do it', swallow questions, obey orders

Stuff doubt down way far down

Complete the mission, bring everyone or most, home safe

The noble warrior vet goes out to make his own or families honest keep

So, the boys and girls, who bear his name, will see he's got what it takes

and smiling proudly, go off to their war

Make you as proud of them as your dad was proud of you

Yet, fight for what? Die for what, De-mockery? … The Rich?

It makes no difference!

Wars have always made generals, businessmen politicians rich while Good

folk and their families suffer the pain, believe in goodness since

To realize their child died in vain would be Unbearable!

The lie wears thin when truth can finally eat a hole big enough to

Finally see we've been suckered into making someone else real rich at
The cost of our Soul, our Life, the Promise of safe, respectful
Descent living!

How many wars all over the world will it take to kill WAR!
Bury Memorial Day
Stop dying to protect the rich lifestyle
The scaling down of society back to the rich and whatever's those
Indentured whites, imprisoned blacks, exiled Latinos along with Whoever
might be left merely laborers at will
For a dime an hour

Been that way since the Rich wrote Their Constitution to fit their fancy
Leggings, jackets, European shoes, snotty top-notch schools to spawn
Another generation of narcissistic, spoiled snot bent on more Destruction,
better destruction, clean, slick video game destruction so More profits
stuff their pockets

Money always needs another enemy within or without to Make more Money!
Make sure those who live beyond rich sound proofed walled communities
kill and die from every shade of horror!

Sorry kids, it's your world now!

The answer to the burning question lies with you!

Are you the ones who will bury Memorial Day?

Winter Afternoon

Winter blows frigid

white tears icy, dust off the tiny lens from whence conscience

peers, seeks goodness but stark landscapes offer nothing

just a winter afternoon, bland in its naked rawness

truth encrusted fingers caught in a death stretch for air

the crunch of booted feet against the silence, only colder

growing while it ages with each passing sigh upon which

the wish that wanted summer heat over, floats laughing

its bony palm slaps my face energized from an arctic gust

Its hands troll the desolate sprawl, cemetery quiet, broken

only by, those steel bottom boots, breaking their way, through winter

each crunch a revolt against nature's turn of season, rejecting

hibernation, since sleep wastes time and wasted time loses

money, and lost money cannot decrease only increase the debt

slowly increasing even with work, rest now a useless commodity

cannot be afforded, what is a body worth without money

i need more coffee, need thicker wool gloves, but

they are out of reach, so only the cheap ones must do for now

the now that extends across a life a chilling plague of death

it's only merit, the sleep that comes with ice, so the moment of

the great punctuation to the sentence of my name will not be

felt only dreamed in the cocoon of winds swirling truth, midst

this, Winter afternoon

Words bend these days

a consequence of riddled truth
speech too full of blood begets lies

we, silent bystanders. caught in the traffic policed by doubt, ignorance
confusion, try to avoid but cannot help but slip, into dark spaces where
irreverent release of anger, pent up genital sludge, grab us by the back
of our necks, drive us left and right, but mostly, empty nowhere

bodies become roads we travel, their lives empty spaces in history
books, so silence commands the frequency of sound
only those rich enough to afford the price, fly far overhead
their clique relieved pops the cork of their little girl or boy champagne

all becomes well regardless of bent words, they don't matter
the only matter, the stock market gets a good goose from the sale of
those tuxedo-ed souls...

"Words play tricks" and "scars shall bleed again"
- Awakened

awakened by the blood from the holes in my back

the ones you made when, i thought you were planting flowers

everlasting flowers since your words kissed me so, so moist

so, to anoint me an ever-holy companion as i splashed in those hot

juicy, erotic streams perfumed with your name

those fragrant sighs night blazing when, you melted from yourself

into the goddess of my dreams, lifted me from death

to massage me back to life, find in you the bed to let my fullness

safely expand, paint you with my joy before, i sank into

deep oblivion, flesh expired, spirit quenched

Awakened yes, when dawn ripped off the blankets from my eyes

gripped my waist with lightening hands, shook me from bleeding into

the other side where, words made no sense, or memories with lips or

teeth made sense of every moment of every piece of time

even the time i thought i had wasted getting off by myself to

relieve the pain, stop the knife from sinking any further into

the heartland, save myself momentarily from suffocation, that slow

unmerciful death that yells names at you with furnace blazing

vengeance, peel back every scar, open every callous over every spider

hole you thought you could hide the dark mean crap that snarled in you

 in me, in the us we tried but could never be, since

The words we spoke were never strong enough to last the test of days
the weather of weeks, even though we meant them at the moment we
held each other as if falling to our death, hoping for the one to save the
other, the other to save the one, only to wake up to the alarm clock and
kiss each other frantically and not remember why
just aggravate each other since neither of us were morning people, yet
could not avoid having to get up early to avoid morning traffic, yes
all that and the words too that this time showed their Othello selves

But you could not stab deep enough, just enough to wound forever
the me i wanted to give to you, despite those desperate moments when
i thought it better to leave and let you call me when you came to yourself
and me to my body, both of us a more sane resemblance of the photos
we carried in our wallets, but
this time, the blood pours
i am weak...
awakened, i cannot move...
i want to, i but cannot move...

i have not given up, it just no longer makes sense to move in anyway
i am tired of the wounds, old and fresh that pour more out of me than
i can pour back in, i have no more strength to drop kick them
off my tongue, watch them smack hard the back of your head so
when you turn you already have teary eyes you cannot hide from me
and blood ran from the slight crack in your skull, that was not as thick
as i thought, and mine neither as hard as you took for granted and kept
pounding even when the referee whistled and kept ringing the bell
and the police came and tried to pull you off me, you were raging strong

pain cleansing, ridding your flesh of stacked up scars

popping them to blast old crap a----way

Far away, deep into the universe of my breath you took as justice

i would too, but you got me first, so i took the words for both of us

and you made the sentence real

awakened turned away with no whistles, fouls or penalties

just left, slammed the door...

period!

Wounds, wounds

What wounds, yes, womb wounds pre-verbal, all watery

sensation, sonic waved watery sharp lips wound in the wake

of their kiss

Already we're bloody before we arrive, so what's new when

when we finally show up, the sound, slur, slap are vaguely old

since the mind interns what's too scary to know, the shock of

the present is enough to take, now let's lose its new wounds

Yet, despite all its clever sleight-of-hand tricks can't keep the old

scary under the dark top hat, sobs spill spark bedtime cries

middle of the night screams uncontained despite all the amusing

ways we try to do AB-BRA-KA-DAB-BRA!

Sooner or later one wises up to forget yesterday's sorrows since

today arrives with its new, improved wounds with rightest

audacity, with the ammo of late night passed congressional deals

that outlaw any rebel, spirit or real, with the military at the

border armed with plenty of ammo, so there's no chance to deal

clean out your pockets there's some new wounds on the way

looks like another Katrina Day!!

There's only you, no life preserver, helicopter rescue, red cross

shelter, St Vincent de Paul church basement food kitchen

there is no basement, just you on the corner, with the bullies
behind, and you waiting for that damned light to change, so
you make the bus, just hear their slurs, curses, and threats that
nail a death sentence notice on tomorrow's door

Every crosswalk light awakens the wound, rips open the scab
let's terror explode, once more you sink a Titanic wound into
a headache sea, till the energy has spent its spleen, or enough
drinks have washed the menace out to sea

Everything had its chance, chance, the almost wound, the winner
of the second-best college, job, home, marriage that spoiled if
not wrecked happiness with its shame stink, that self-inflicted
catholic penance of unworthiness, each lash a confirmation of
your unredeemable sinner-hood fated to purgatory condemned
in this life and all others--Amen!

When only your car's parked in the driveway, your friends dead
and your marriage too, its bleak for sure, cause in the gray time
all the wounds come home to roost, and all the kids are gone
except, the doorbell rings, your youngest daughter just happens
to be in town and thought to stop by for a visit, plants a kiss on
your barnyard stumble cheek, a hug around your slightly bent
shoulders, out of the blue, tenderly speaks:

"Daddy, i just want to thank you for all that you've done and
provided for us, though you were gone a lot and i missed you so
cried a lot but got over it, found enough of myself and carried on

was always happy to see you no matter how long, because you
were and are my Dad!

i realized you could only do your best with the cards you were
dealt since i faced the same challenge, was wounded enough
watched what others went through, learned the lessons no
textbook or business class can teach, just accept the fact that life is
full of all different kinds of light or heavy wounds, their pain
can linger if you let it, but it didn't take long for me to realize that
holding on to it doesn't help make things better, if some sting
remains, just let it know you know, soon it will go away because
it knows it can't hurt you anymore, those that stay seem to
mellow with age, i'm not that old, but that's happened already to
me, their sting turns mellow, their once sadistic revenge, gone

Don't worry Daddy, you can always call, the key is still under
the front door mat, a pot of coffee on stand-by, the past is past, it
does not belong in the present, the happy does, the good stuff
does, the other stuff can rest like sleeping dogs, today has its
worth to be felt and lived, tomorrow comes too soon becomes
today and like you used to say: 'Come on now, it's a new
day! Let's not spoil breakfast!'"

You are a mystery

i am also, one to myself, along with the world

can wonder for a moment stop

concern can't do 2 things at once

i can or used to before a slight bomb went off

in my brain, changed the landscape of my life to

a table for 1

It is all mystery

we can only go so far before the road collapses

into a frenzy of spooked questions

mystery will do that to your ego

You are in another world, enveloped with neither

address nor postage in a cloud of unknowing

everything i learned dissolved a waste product good

for only a working toilet and a quick flush to make

sure, nothing got up & out but went down all the way

down w/o any chance to crawl out on behalf of its own

aliveness, only to be murdered, its stubborn will

wanting to exist, an almost unkillable energy except

when 2 hands get clamped around its neck and squeeze

then and only then Sunday goes to bed forever since

at last, a + b = the square root of pi x r squared – q

The 2nd year is always the worst, the first is full of rumors
easily squashed, you get used to it, but the 2nd year is a
constant waterboarding

i couldn't wait for Friday then Sunday night make my
forehead burn so my mother would call in sick for me
Monday at 8:05 am precisely

My father never believed me, for years he questioned
my pedigree since my handwriting never matched his
how perplexed and anorexic he turned after the DNA
test proved him false and my mother took the house
with her when she returned to somewhere in Northern
Europe to die in a supposed ski accident 3 and a 1/3 yrs. later

When my father heard the news, he swallowed his tongue
and died, i swear the sky opened up for him, then spit him
out into the Atlantic Ocean

The mystery, his, mine, ours, the one we want to solve
know, hug, kiss, love, as if its final autopsy would
solve every question, answer every ache, pay off every
student loan w/enough left over for a descent car to get
from Western MA to Seattle

Don't ask me why i need a mystery
my life is not complete w/o it, i need it to distract my-
self, a night of full sleep would ruin my next day, it could

make me sick, since i was no longer in turmoil

Come onnnnn! don't try to reason with me, everything
is in turmoil, we eat it, sleep in it, get up and wash in it
dress up in it, drive through it
how come people drive the way they do? they are in
turmoil, if you don't get into it, you'll get killed
you don't want that, it's not the way to go! there's no
Twitter in that, everybody jamming Fb with their
flower arrangement memories of you, at least for
one day!

Don't look at me like i am capitulating to a less than A+
blow job because i'm tired, it's only the turmoil, the turmoil
i choose to call mystery, why? Because i'm a Poet!
i have to make things sound and taste different, toss it a bit
so, you don't know what's next, if you think you do
you'll get a surprise smack!! HA!!
i do it so i eat some vegetables at least once a day, satisfy my
dead mother

Mystery sounds holy, if you don't need it, at least it offers a
semblance of holy, ok, don't use it, i don't care, don't worry
i'm not gonna jam it down your throat with a fork! Alright?
i'll use the "T" word around you, but it won't change how i
feel about the erotic sense the new underwear i just bought gives me
i feel like i'm 28 again, and so full of mystery, even i don't
know myself so don't ask-

i couldn't answer then, and since hell hasn't frozen over
yet, can't answer now, so let's have another and dance
it's only mystery… You do realize it could be a lot worse
we could really know the actual monster we are, plus the
history of murders that flow–through our Purex white veins

i don't think you are anywhere close to being able to live
that real… i thought so… O-Kaaaaaaaaay!
order another round, kick off your shoes and dance, i ½
promise not to step on your bleeding hoofs

"You go to church on Sunday: I go to humanity everyday," he proclaimed

Yes, what is left of humanity
the pulse that fuels mine, the connection that offers food
the word that arrives by thunder to keep me awake, so i do not
miss the hurt to the smallest relation of my human aliveness

Offer my arms for it to find a home, some kind of healing, if only the
touch that brings recognition to one almost erased by the arrogant world
marching without looking, marching without care, marching for its own
opulence, marching for its own gain

The more it wants to put into its own bulging pockets, regardless
of the cost of poverty, neglect, murder of all who may fall beneath
the shadow of its marching

Let me embrace humanity
i have had enough of the empty bluster of those
supposed collared copies of god
who walk down streets eying only the landscapes of themselves

Your words paint such wonderful images

they pull me in to the place you are walking, eating, siting, park bench
reflecting, faking nose blowing while instead you are about picking

before i know it, i free fall without a sigh or yell for help
i am there wherever you are and so alive
i am electric, and i am not plugged in
just walking on my own two pins
without worry or wobble or wince

i am 55 again!! and loving it
a nice honey on my arm would be icing on the cake, but
we are walking too loose to not gain
we have enough on these frail bones bold with poetry
don't want to lose any hot lines from over indulgence
we are too young to trip down into that night!...

we will go dancing with enchiladas for you and
peanut butter sandwiches for me with a whole case of our favorite
wine to make sure we will have enough inspiration
to get us safely to those pearly gates and step over
if anyone is there to answer the doorbell!

Your Words Electric

catch a deep vibe, fine-tuned searching for its home

somewhere between concrete sidewalk - asphalt street

crying child - grandma's holy lap

later, the place at the end of distance, sugar candy stretched

enough to keep you satisfied but always starving for more

yes, an optimism that just misses the crash into the bleak

the place too many get stuck

the place you just find bones of what hoped to be

no one remains alive, so, possibly with the dance

we can find the smooth to get around just fine enough

to make it enough, to make it good enough and smile when

the lights go out, glad just to know the best of whatever

could be, was gotten in the nick of time!

21st Century Requiem Love

The day broke through the window

a blonde chick with a broken heel

½ dressed curses clawed me up from mattress rancid sleep, worse

than that Damned alarm clock

Huh, what's time when i've thrown up your eternity

hmmmmm… space the ravaged landscape of your purr

no matter how hard you dream the next moment will bring heaven

Hellllllllllllllllllllllllllllllllllllllllllllllllllllllllllll

don't U yell at Me

i didn't wreck your shoe

you stepped into a hole tighter than yours

not my fault

i told you to avoid gin but you had to play bingo on somebody's lap

Oh… a revenge card nailed to my forehead, yeah, i found it alright

as if that could ever make a difference

nah, you couldn't wait for me to find the tingling key to salvation

i can't blame you, belief is just a dick slap in the face

Well, get over here, i am your physician

let me soothe with my tongue your panty less lips, you

brought back to me; make everything… better

i'm close, just wait, you'll have an axis to steady your Argentina

both of us Will sink beneath those sheets

where asses and armpits write their histories

make room to bang that T-rex gong

Maxwell hammer, ginger baker high, those

sweet round moons as our shadows spread their eclipse

turn them blood red sweaty howls

i will moisten your dangling lanterns a blaze of screaming flames

while you farm my neck with your apocalyptic teeth

dig my back a garden for your snapdragons

i'll revise the chapters of your book of revelations, beloved

behind window blinded day

Your wake-up call a penance i will deliver

until our oils have spilled all our tattoos

enchantment a broken lighter leaves our last cigarettes lifeless

until the flesh for that great AAAAAAAAAAAA – HA- HAMEN

collapses a pile of ashes

a cool death to feed on each other

till full

we will rise back into each other's arms

no matter where we have traveled

whether the moon shines or…Not

When the taco falls apart

from the distance chimes sound a lovely melody
i forget the loss, slip into the serenity of luscious sound
fullness warm embraced

i recline upon the floor of memory, dusty with all kinds of
diapers, faint tears, lost home works, lovers at the playground
fights over the seesaw, or whatever we did or did not see

Before great waves of unawareness swept us apart
swam us to all sorts of grand adventures, surprising places
wanted and unwanted bed partners as the days turned into weddings
weddings turned into homesteads, time into the labor of paying for
a life that required no more than simply a hug of recognition
the kiss of affection to seal the thought that i was still worth
being here, still loved regardless of all the scrapes and bruises
bills and missed promises
despite the grayness of landscapes once verdant fields of
pleasure promises ever blossoming

Still it is just the taco on the floor, not me, not now, not yet
bells have yet to toll my name, sweep my bones from
jump rope games, hopscotch filled streets, my pulsing dreams
Despite everything, i still love the was, is, the might be
the will be, along with the tacos that still fall apart!

beneath this gray day

i find myself a puddle
that tiny lake holds me as if my real mother
there i feel warm despite the wind that shakes the pine tree tops
slaps tree branches up and around
like them i am awakened, but not by slaps of wind
the voice of one whispering my name as morning sprouts legs
begins to walk into noon mountains, leaves us alone
the water and i
to figure out our own problems together, the way the young
that is older and the older that is suddenly young meet beneath
the shade of an autumn blush
mysterious contours of love suddenly shape-shift
bench hard, pillow soft, almost too talkative, like a nervous
telephone call full of too many conversations not
listening to yet still, miraculously, hearing each other
so magical, almost hard to believe, love, the work of heart
only needs the mind to work out the practical details about
money, a safe place to sleep, survival of sorts not just on kisses
or sweet dreams and lollipops, so kindergarten, yet still so
wanted, even when time has proved them seldom to
even exist, remain the number one and two wished for items
among the majority of those in every decade of age extending
almost to100, alas, not quite, if not actually to have
since we rarely get that chance in the real sphere of the

the actual world, we wind up obnoxiously back in, despite our

prayers and all the kicking and tears, curses and bribes, lies

and entreaties for re-negotiations, that never worked for

the mortgage, so why our lives, tangled up in each other like

kittens caught up in a pile of yarn

between the water and i, earth and sky, her open dancing eyes

my patched-up screened in porch, her youth with stretch, my

breath with short elastic slippers you can hear a mile away

scratching the kitchen floor, magic blossoms!

a garden unbelievable, grand, so fantastically alive she can't believe it

i want to hold on to it for as long as my fingers can without cramping up

breaking off into the outer space of history

since, the fire burns, feels itself ecstatic and she unburdened

seeks mature grounded arms to be there, loyal, constant, one with

knowledge not just fast talk, quick fever, in the front door, out the

back, no working out some freudian slip or jungian fairy tale

only mellowed affection to finally rock gently through the storm

stand guard since he has had longer night sojourns into dark

nightmares, slayed those nasty dragons that burnt the cup cakes

a few beloved dreams, but not harmed too deep the precious life that

gives it self so freely, not just to please but be the gift desired, the one

to still complete something, patch some rip that flaps a grief that needs

to be kissed, mended with the holding only few can give in return, yet

somehow know from birth, read by the feel of looks, touch of words

the temperature of silences, the weather of eyes that cannot find the

words to speak, only trace the problem with tears, and nether be

afraid but ever present, it's the being there that sees, and feels, even if

it has no answer, an answer may not be the answer, just being there counts, so one is no longer in some darkness alone, but beneath a gray day, a puddle one can float on, or when the clock strikes the last chime simply dissolve, without regret, into the depths always wanted to be tasted

noontime

how are you at noontime?

high as the sun, shining your most

a wave surfing on its dreams

a thought on tree limb just musing time away in splendid reverie

slow chewing a sandwich to get the most out of your naira

a face on elbow drifting out your bedroom window

wishing on candles simmering behind your eyes

the ones that make you smile when, things get too dark, so

that cuts the dark a bit, so suddenly you see through the

problem to the answer, or at least a good enough one

one that will sooth if not satisfy, since

isn't that what noon is about, the sooth, that

break in the commotion, that coming up for air

that going to the rest room, just to take a walk, since

outside is not that good, too full of nasty

too mucked up with dis-ease

there's enough of that

it's noontime, time for the sooth to satisfy

knit everything slowly back together with a gentle smile

that cares and almost doesn't at the same time

like the child thinking she got something over on the teacher

when the teacher is outside looking for a better switch for

you know who

but that is later and later is not now

it's the now of noontime and

i am in hammock softly swaying to some noontime smooth

are you?

Jeff Cannon: A U.S. New England poet, author of
Intimate Witness: The Carol Poems (Goose River Press, 2009),
Eros Faces of Love and Finding the Father at Table (X-Libris, 2010).

I was an ever-present attendee (until recently due to health issues)
at the "Dirty Gerund Poetry Show" at Ralph's Diner.
It is the place that became my poetry home to celebrate music
and the gifts of many young poets and musicians.

Other publishing credits include Goose River Anthology
(2009 & 2014) and Boundless 2014 & 2020 (El Zarape Press).